£4.95

GROWING UP IN CARE

The Practice of Social Work

General editors: Bill Jordan and Jean Packman

Growing Up in Care

Ten People Talking

BARBARA KAHAN

Basil Blackwell • Oxford

First published 1979 by
Basil Blackwell Publisher
5 Alfred Street
Oxford OX1 4HB
England

British Library Cataloguing in Publication Data

Kahan, Barbara
    Growing up in care.—(The practice of social
    work series).
    1. Children - Institutional care - England -
History - 20th century
    I. Title II. Series
    362.7'32'0942 HV887.G5

ISBN 0 631 12171 4
ISBN 0 631 12161 7 Pbk

TO VLADIMIR

Reproduced from copy supplied
printed and bound in Great Britain
by Billing and Sons Limited
Guildford, London, Oxford, Worcester

Contents

Foreword

EILEEN YOUNGHUSBAND

We have tried as never before in the last thirty years to devise effective services to help those who for one reason or another at some time in their lives cannot cope by themselves. Yet astonishingly it is only in the last ten years or so that we have begun to ask the clients themselves what they thought about the help we gave them. Great efforts were, and are, made in the best public and voluntary services to make the right responses to need, to make the services more flexible and sensitive to individual differences. A great deal of imagination, much personal devotion and objective observation has gone into this. But too often it has been assumed that those who provided the services knew best, so that there was no need to ask the wearer of the shoe where it pinched.

Yet only those going through any experience can know how it feels, and, after all, how it feels to them is how it *is* to them. This book records the first attempt, fewer than ten years ago, to consult a group of men and women who grew up in the care of a local authority children's department about what the experience was like from their point of view. The author, Barbara Kahan, formerly Children's Officer for Oxfordshire County Council, initiated and ran the discussion group. This was only one of the many imaginative activities for which she was responsible and which made the Department a pioneer in good standards of child care.

It is especially important to try to discover either at the

time or later how the experience of growing up in care affects
a child because a child's world is different, both more vivid
and more powerless, than an adult's world, and because some
happenings of childhood can set their stamp for life. One of
the most striking things about this book is the contrast
between the benign adults so carefully planning for each
individual child's well-being and the child's own sense of
separateness and aloneness, of fear, of uncertainty about
what was going to happen in the future, and the sense of
being at the mercy of houseparents, foster parents and child
care officers. These were usually kind and concerned but they
did not care about the child in any ultimate sense, "my
Tommy right or wrong", and they might come and go all too
rapidly.

These group discussions bring out with a sharp immediacy
how the child's image of himself and his world could be
splintered by the shock of removal from his home. The still
fluid sense of identity, so much part of familiar people and
surroundings, is thrown into confusion, and as a consequence
the child withdraws into himself in self-protection: "Fear
gives you a blind which you pull down". And then there is
the hazard that real communication will not be established
again. The discussions show that this knitting together of the
sundered past with the present and the unknown future is
perhaps the central problem in providing good substitute
care, good parenting say the group, coming to the heart of
the problem. To provide this is something far harder than to
ensure good physical care. They stress that what the child
craves, but is wary of trusting, is someone to whom he will
matter as his individual self, to whom he can talk freely, who
will understand and stand by him but who will also care
enough to say "no" as well as "yes" and who will make
demands upon him. Out of the window goes the professional
relationship as a sufficient alternative, in which every child is
treated alike, and children are related to the department
rather than to individuals. Out of the window go rapid staff
changes, or changes for the child himself, and anything which

distinguishes the Homes children from other children. The group discussions brought out the children's intense desire to be just like other children — and other children's cruelty to those who are not.

What these ten men and women treasured as their best memories were the staff or foster parents who had been kind, patient and understanding, who stopped to listen, who helped them to sort out tangles and problems and to come to terms with their lives, who were firm but gentle. The group agreed that every child in care should have someone who was able to act as an encouraging and special person, to confide in and to give comfort in distress. Of course there are very many children in their own homes who do not have this, or sometimes do not realize until long afterwards the richest gift of childhood that was missing. Yet this lack matters more to children who have suffered the loss of their own families and homes.

Perhaps what the group says we knew in a general rather blurred way, perhaps too we tend to deny it because we cannot face the child's pain. The group, and others like them, have it in their power to open our eyes; they talk far more effectively than most text books because here the sharp impact of direct experience is re-lived. The members of the group were a selected, because self-selected, group of men and women who are making their own way in life, often in marriage and in bringing up their own children. Their ability to do this is largely due to what they were given and were able to receive from the child care service, from its strengths and in spite of its weaknesses. What they have to say makes all the more difficult the task in child care and we need their help and that of others like them to do it better. For example, how can we discover, recruit, support and retain in the service of children in care people with the capacity to be the reliable, understanding adult whom the group is undoubtedly right in saying each individual child should have?

Preface

In her latest book, *Social Work in Britain 1950-1975*,[1] Eileen Younghusband speaks of the "unfinished agenda" of Children's Departments which were brought into being in 1948 and ceased to exist in 1971, when they were absorbed into Social Services Departments. This book may perhaps be seen as part of that unfinished agenda.

It is also in some senses the payment of a debt; a debt to a group of ten people who were willing at the author's request to discuss their childhoods in public care and how they felt about the service provided for them. The ten people had all been in care for long periods, none for less than five years, and some for almost eighteen. They were all in care when they reached their eighteenth birthday and some had received continuing help after that date. They were part of the hard core of long stay cases which formed a large part of any children's department's responsibilities. Children's departments from their inception had the task of providing substitute care for children from birth to eighteen years of age for any period of time ranging from a day or two to the whole of their first eighteen years of life. Each year since 1948 many thousands of children have been received into care and many thousands discharged. Many of those discharged were short-stay cases, the same children who shortly before had been admitted; but amongst the total in care on any day of the year there was always a high proportion of children who had remained in care for a long period. From 1948 until 1977 the annual official statistics did not disclose how many there were. Some local authorities were able to determine the numbers from their own records. Others with less adequate records were not. Occasionally a piece of research cast light on the size and some of the characteristics of this group, e.g. the Social Survey Study in 1957 on "Children in Care and the Recruitment of Foster Parents"[2] found that on any given day 40 per cent of children had been in care for over five years.

Eighteen hundred children were studied and then classified according to the original reasons for their admission and the circumstances which then gave rise to long-term care. Fit person orders (now care orders) from juvenile courts accounted for 25 per cent of the total sample. Loss of parents by death or abandonment accounted for 15 per cent, homelessness for 10 per cent, illegitimacy for 9 per cent and deserting mothers for 8 per cent. By contrast, confinements and short-term illnesses of parents, which accounted for very high numbers of annual admissions to care, accounted for only 2 per cent and 3 per cent respectively of long-term care cases.

A further research study, "Child Care: Needs and Numbers" by Jean Packman,[3] carried out between 1960 and 1964, gave further information about children in long-stay care. Fifty local authorities were studied, of which forty-two completed questionnaires over a six-month period on every application for admission to care whether the child was admitted or not and for every fit person order made by the courts during the same period. A total of 4,500 questionnaires were completed. Child care officers were asked to estimate how long the children involved in applications were likely to remain in care if admitted and it was assumed that children committed on fit person orders were likely to be in long-term care. The difference between the sorts of situations which might be expected to create long-term problems on the one hand and short-term problems on the other were clearly seen. In the first place long-term cases were seen to be more complex, with proportionately more reasons for admission than short-term cases. There was more than one reason for care given in 50 per cent of long-term

compared with 28 per cent of short-term cases. The broken or
incomplete family was the dominant characteristic of long-
term cases. In 52 per cent of admissions the lack of a parent
or parents was given as the major reason for long-term care,
and more than a third of the contributory reasons for care
also fell under this heading. The special vulnerability of the
family unit that was incomplete or broken was also shown in
information about the identity of persons caring for the
children at the time application for care was made to the
children's departments. Only 46 per cent of all families
concerned were at that time simple units of natural mother,
father and children. When admissions to long-term care were
analysed, the proportion of intact families, i.e. with both
mother and father living at home, fell to 21 per cent. At the
time of Jean Packman's study short term cases, that is, those
of under six months' duration, the definition used in statistics
published by the Home Office Children's Department,
accounted for between 6 and 7 per cent only on March 31st in
any year.

Recently published statistics, Children in Care in England
and Wales, 1977,[4] for the first time provide information
nationally about the duration of episodes of care. They show
that although 52,100 children were admitted to care and
49,300 discharged during the period April 1st 1976 to March
31st 1977, on March 31st 1977 26,900 had been in care for
more than five years, 6,900 for less than five years but more
than three and 33,400 for less than three years but more than
one year, a total in all of approximately 75 per cent in care for
more than one year. In the year ending March 31st 1977,
7,500 were discharged from care having reached eighteen
years of age and a further 600 were discharged at nineteen
years old under provisions dating from the Children and
Young Persons Act 1969.

The research studies referred to above and the recent
national statistics demonstrate a fact that can easily be lost
sight of in the urgency and pressure of thousands of children
flowing in and out of care every year. The fact is that since

1948 local authorities have had to provide long-term care for a very large number of children and young people, now around 75,000 on any one day. This is essentially a different task from providing substitute parental care for a few days or weeks while mothers are confined or ill or during other brief emergencies. The differences increase the longer the periods of time become. For the longest of the long-term cases virtually total upbringing of a child is the task. This then poses the question of how this can be achieved in view of the demands of human growth and development in the first two decades of life and the emotional needs which are not lessened, but increased, by the loss of what children in normal family circumstances can take for granted in security, attachment, continuity of care and nurture and all that goes with these.

Children's departments were established in 1948 as the best way the Curtis Committee could suggest to provide "for children who from loss of parents or from any cause whatever are deprived of a normal home life with their own parents or relatives."[5] As Eileen Younghusband put it:

The task in 1948 was to work a sea change in the care given to children deprived of a normal home life, and to discover what good substitute care for individual children might mean. . . . . . When the children's departments came to an end in 1971, great strides had been made since 1948 in clarifying the needs of children actually or potentially deprived of nurturing relationships, and of children with behaviour problems which resulted in efforts to provide similarly for the deprived and the delinquent. Translated into operational terms this included discovering what should be the nature of preventive services, good residential care, fostering and adoption, though much remained to be discovered, applied and tested. . . . . . It is strange that in a field where so much was at stake there should have been . . . no publicly sponsored, large-scale research into various aspects of family welfare and child care. Thus in some departments crucial decisions could depend on individual, unverified experience and opposing values not put to the test of objective inquiry, while in other departments there was careful work and discussion amongst colleagues. Throughout the period there was a striking difference between the standards achieved by different local authorites.[6]

Not only was there no publicly sponsored, large-scale research, but there were also few or no consumer reaction studies. That is, the services did not, in general, seek to discover how those they cared for felt about the care they received, nor what effect it had on their later life as adults after they left care. Such research as there has been may even, because of its partial nature, have given a false picture of the results of a public upbringing. Much research into aspects of the penal system, for example, shows that it is not uncommon for the prison and borstal populations to contain numbers of men who have spent periods of time in the care of local authorities and voluntary organizations when they were children. Other research, much of it directed towards establishments which have sheltered or contained young offenders, has cast considerable doubt on the efficacy of residential work as a form of substitute care and remedial management. But these are essentially minority situations compared with the army of people in the community who for a period of time in their childhood must have had to rely on public resources for the basic upbringing needed during the years of dependency.

Taking into account normal life expectancy, the number of people working, marrying, producing children, living out their lives in the community who have had this experience must be very considerable. It is now accepted without question that the years of childhood influence adults for the rest of their lives, and yet policy concerning the services, the allocation of resources, the methods employed in looking after children whose own families cannot do so, owe little to first-hand knowledge of how those people themselves felt about the experience and how it affected them.

Awareness of how important this firsthand knowledge might be was the motivation behind the discussions which form the basis of this book. The author's first tentative attempts at discovering how some children in care felt about their experience are described and the steps which led to the more detailed and organized discussions with a group of former children in care, then adults.

It is important to make explicit the aims and limitations of what was attempted. The number of people involved, ten, was very small. They came because they were invited or volunteered and their participation was evidence of identification with the purpose of the group. They understood that for these reasons they were not necessarily, in any regard, typical of people who as children had spent long periods in public care. On the other hand, it is equally not possible necessarily to say that in any regard they were untypical; it was just not possible to know. Nor was the work carried out with them dependent on their being either typical or untypical. It was not a research study based on a sample, however limited. It was only a small attempt with a small group to learn a little about what it felt like to them to have been in care and to see whether what emerged might be of value in increasing the sensitivity of services for other children by identifying issues or problems which had been significant to the group. The author's previous attempts to do this had mainly been with boys and girls who were on the point of leaving care at eighteen years of age. At this point some had been through a stormy adolescence, similar to the stage through which many young people in their own homes pass in their late teens, but often made more difficult by their major losses of natural supports, their anxiety about themselves and their future and frustrations caused by many unmet needs. Some had had less stormy passages but were inevitably still in that stage of development when adult life has yet to be experienced.

Their reactions to what had happened or was still happening to them were therefore more immediate, less reflective and lacking the sense of proportion which further experience might later provide in some instances. By contrast the group assembled by the author in 1970 had passed beyond the official boundary into adult life, some very recently, some long enough to have had several years in which to realize the responsibilities it carries with it and to be seeing childhood through the perspective of their own children's lives. They had all had the experience of having to stand fully on their own feet, maintain themselves and test out how far their upbringing in public care had helped or hindered them in doing so.

The method used in discussion was simple and relatively unstructured. A series of topics was selected by the group and one of these was used at each meeting to start discussion. On a number of occasions the topic for the next meeting was agreed beforehand so that group members were able to do a little preparatory thinking, and aid recall by so doing. Very occasionally a professional member of the group, the children's officer or one of the two colleagues who worked with her, contributed an experience with a child or family which fitted into the pattern of the subject for discussion. This was seldom necessary, however, because the group members rapidly demonstrated their capacity to contribute to a fluent and free-flowing discussion in which the professional members only had to offer the occasional explanation or comment, or to pull one or two points together, to assist the general development. The pattern of meetings was consistent throughout, and the main structures imposed were selection of topics, pre-arranged dates and a consistent time geared to the constraints of the group members' family, work and weekend responsibilities. It became clear by about the ninth meeting that the time allowed by the two last meetings arranged for 1970 would probably be sufficient to allow adequate discussion of the remaining topics and issues which the group had considered important. There was, therefore, some discussion of bringing the meetings to an end and it was agreed that after the last discussion day there would be a social occasion arranged during the Christmas or early New Year period which would provide an acceptable way of saying goodbye for people who, by that time, had developed a considerable degree of warmth towards each other and mutual support. The last recorded discussions took place at the eleventh regular meeting and any material which emerged during buffet lunches at the eleven meetings or on the social occasion which terminated the group's existence was not recorded.

The material recorded comprises the group's total discussions over approximately thirty-five to thirty-eight hours. It represents memories, impressions, feelings, opinions and some speculation by group members, based on their own experiences whilst in care and later, about how services might be improved. Because it represents memories, impressions, feelings and opinions, like all such human material, it is not always completely accurate. Memories are often distorted by emotion, by partial perception or understanding at the time and by the sifting process of the passing years. Nevertheless what was recalled represents what was significant to the receivers of the services, the people to whom things happened, as distinct from the memories, intentions or records of those people who were instrumental in making things happen. It was in some senses "emotion recollected in tranquillity"[7] though there were times during the discussions when the feelings of an individual member or the group as a whole were powerful as they recalled the past. Perhaps the most poignant of these was when Anne was describing what she recalled of her early childhood, the loss of her mother and her little sister, and her long-standing grief, her later sorrow at leaving the staff she loved in her children's Home, and the unhappiness and frustration of her foster home. Every member of the group, in his or her own way, spoke with what had been, to the children's officer and her colleagues, unexpected vividness and clarity. They themselves had wondered initially what they would be able to say; "I mean I had nothing outstanding happen to me. I thought it all worked out very well, I'd have nothing to say at all," one of them confessed. But when they began to remember and to talk some of the expressions they used to describe their feelings and situations were memorable to those who heard them spoken. For example, "keeping my face up"; "fear gives you a blind which you pull"; "split into a thousand fragments"; "the other side of the grass"; "now I am my own responsibility", were phrases used to describe feelings of determination to be brave, feelings of anxiety in the face of the unknown, being shattered by adult decisions which would not be reversed, the sense of isolation at being "different", the satisfaction of no longer being in care.

Anne was able above all, in a few words, to convey her memories as though the events she recalled were actually happening, and on the occasion described above, the flow of sympathy and understanding from every member of the group was evidenced by their expressions of deep attention and the tears in their eyes as they listened. She felt the warmth and support they gave and later told one of the professional members that it was the first time for some years that she had been able to gain comfort by talking about her feelings to people whom she knew understood and identified with her.

The method used in preparation of this book was essentially one of drawing together material from all the discussions under headings which would concentrate it on certain themes. It would have been possible to assemble it differently and inevitably choices, which may not always have been the most appropriate, had to be made about where a particular passage or discussion best fitted. What can be said is that all the material of any significance has been used. Editing has been concentrated on eliminating repetition, making the sense clear where necessary (sometimes by a few words in brackets which are the author's) and providing a framework for presentation which enables, as far as possible, a flow of thought to be followed. There has been no selection in any other senses than these. The bulk of the text is either in the form of direct quotation from members of the group, or, where it seemed more appropriate, paraphrasing a passage or passages of discussion to bring out the main points without loss of anything but the conversational surplus which is likely to be part of any discussion. It was intended from the outset that the main emphasis of the book should be the ten people talking, and the three professional members have therefore been kept in the background. The children's officer is referred to throughout in the third person and neither she nor her two professional colleagues have been given names. All three saw themselves as facilitators in the work being carried out and the tapes when typed demonstrated clearly the relatively small part played by them in the discussions. The group as a whole was a heart-warming experience for them and appeared to be so for all the members. Although feelings were sometimes strong, in contemplation of what had happened or might still happen, the attitudes of members to each other were courteous, helpful, understanding and considerate. They gave their full attention to each other and were quick to respond and comment constructively and with sensitivity. On no occasion was there any awkwardness or tension and the general atmosphere was relaxed and supportive to everyone. The ten people whose experience had been asked for appeared confident in offering it and were not, as the text will show, inhibited from commenting critically, not only on matters for which some responsibility was held by people who were not present, but also on matters for which the children's officer or her two colleagues were directly responsible. An example of this was Miranda's comments on the children's officer's refusal to let her leave her boarding school. But this was not the only evidence of their ability to say what they felt about what had happened. They believed they were providing something of value and were happy to be able to do so.

They also saw the group itself as something of value to them and made a proposal during the discussions that other similar groups should be set up all over the country. They proposed this for two reasons: the first, that it could provide more opportunities to enlarge understanding by those responsible for social services of the problems of children in care, and in consequence lead to improvements in services for children; the second, that people who had been in care as children might have opportunities to discuss their experiences with other people who would understand and thus help them to come to terms with some of their unresolved residual problems. At the time the group was meeting such opportunities were unlikely to be found anywhere, unless by the kind of chance which led to their own group. Clients' groups were characteristic of methods of work in some branches of psychiatry and some social work, but the author had not then, nor since, heard of similar groups of people who had been in care until the initiative taken by the National Children's Bureau in 1975 when the "Who Cares?" Conference was organized. This was an opportunity for young people living in care at that time to come together and "speak freely about what mattered to them most."[8] The Bureau stated that its action had been "prompted by the recognition of the fact that since the end of the war it has been increasingly accepted that institutionalized forms of public care present serious obstacles to the satisfactory social, emotional and educational development of children. . . . Very little work has been done to find out what the children themselves think of the life that society has provided for them."[9] The one-day conference involved twenty-eight local authorities and two agencies who sent one hundred children between the ages of twelve and sixteen years. Subsequently a Young People's Working Group was established and a report published in 1977. Since then a number of similar groups have been formed in various parts of the country. The ten people talking together in 1970 would have welcomed such a development and would have supported the "Who Cares?" Young People's Working Group who co-opted into membership, amongst their eight adult helpers, four who themselves had grown up in care. From their deliberations they formulated "a charter of rights for young people in care and the things we want to change." Although as far as the author of this book knows none of the group which was meeting in 1970 has ever met the "Who Cares?" group which was meeting in 1976 they would find if they did that they had a great deal in common in the issues and problems which each regarded as important. The fact that there is a strong common element in the views of a group of adults talking in 1970 about their life in public care at various times from about 1942 to 1969 and a group of twelve to sixteen-year-olds talking and writing in 1976 suggests that there are still major problems to be worked out in the provision of care for children "deprived of a normal home life" in 1979 and the 1980s. The problems with which this book is concerned are particularly those of long-stay children who have to depend on public bodies for the provision of substitute parenting during significant periods of their lives. Ten people talking may serve as a reminder of some of those problems. They may perhaps even speak to the concerns of some children in similar situations who are in the same state of bewilderment and anxiety that they were themselves years ago.

Whatever purpose this book may serve I am indebted to many people whose work or contribution has helped me. The ten people whom I have called Alex, Andrew, Anne, Barry, Carol, Derek, Margaret, Martin, Miranda and Valerie gave their time and themselves generously and had confidence that their material would be of value. To work with them was a remarkable experience for which I was and am very grateful. My colleagues Bridget Fann and Anne Collins assisted me in planning for the group and in working with it. They were at every meeting and their professional skill and knowledge were invaluable, not only at the meetings but also in helping members of the group who wished to have personal discussions outside of the meetings. My thanks are also due to Miss D. Graeme-Thomson, who was chairman of the local authority children's committee at the time and who warmly supported the proposal to form a group and use local authority premises and staff in so doing. The meetings would have been the poorer if welcoming refreshments and delicious home-cooked buffet lunches had not been available. For the preparation of those I am indebted to Mrs Howard who worked in her spare time to cook them and also gave up eleven Saturday mornings in 1970 so that we could enjoy an attractively served meal. One other member of the department concerned gave his support and help in a variety of problems which, unsolved, would have handicapped our work. Stanley Summerfield became a friend of the group members as he was of many children in care. His exceptional work over many years and his commitment to the children and his colleagues were such that those who had the privilege of knowing and working with him will always regret his untimely death in 1977.

For the preparation of the records of the discussions, and the text of this book, I am indebted to Grace Foreshew, Diana Tutt and Mrs Templeton, all of whom patiently worked their way through transcripts or drafts with good humour, efficiency and speed.

I am grateful to Jean Packman who listened to all the tapes, read the transcripts and encouraged me to believe that the group's discussions might be of value to social work teachers. My husband, as ever, has patiently discussed, listened, read and re-read and, most difficult of all, acted as a candid critic.

Finally, I am indebted to the many colleagues with whom I worked in child care, who shared their knowledge and skill with me, and to the children and young people who taught us all through their infinite variety, resilience and youthfulness and their general tolerance of us and our mistakes.

The flaws and weaknesses of the book are mine.

1 The Setting

This book concerns ten people who met together as a group and talked about some of their experiences as children and adolescents. The common factor between them was that they had been brought up for the whole or a significant part of their first eighteen years in the care of a local authority children's department and had been invited by the children's officer of that department to discuss with her and two of her colleagues their consumer views of the services provided for them. Much of the content of the book is drawn verbatim from these discussions which took place in 1970 when the youngest of the ten was nineteen years old and the oldest thirty-four. It was the last year of a specialized child care service which had been established in 1948 and was about to be merged, along with other personal social services for the elderly, the mentally ill and the mentally and physically handicapped, in unified social services departments following the implementation in law of the Seebohm Committee's main recommendations.[1]

The post-war period in England had produced many changes in public services, not least amongst those provided for children "deprived of a normal home life"[2] with their own parents. Before 1948 four central government departments, the Ministries of Health, Education and Pensions and the Home Office were concerned with deprived children. In local authorities the Health, Education and Public Assistance Committees each had responsibilities for certain groups, and in addition voluntary organizations of many kinds inter-related with the local authorities or worked

1

independently providing services for the same or similar situations of need. This network had developed piecemeal over many years. It provided "much scope for inconsistency of treatment"[3] and had been subjected to pressure by wartime conditions and shortage of manpower. As a consequence of demand for reform[4] and public enquiry into individual disasters[5] the Curtis Committee was appointed in 1945 to examine existing services and make recommendations for the future. Its report supplied a blueprint for the Act which followed.[6] The Committee attributed many of the past inadequacies in child care services to the administrative chaos which had developed through the operation of numerous departments of central and local government and sought to improve the basic structure of the services by simplification and unification of the administrative machinery. In addition they recommended a new and specialized service for children, supported by training for field and residential social workers and personalized in the way it was administered and provided. They had been shocked by evidence of the unimaginative and insensitive handling of many deprived children and were "increasingly impressed by the need for the personal element in the care of children, which Sir Walter Monckton emphasized in his report on the O'Neill case."[7] The appointment of children's officers, in charge of the new children's departments they recommended, was seen by the Committee as "our solution of the problem referred to us."[8] A *Times* leader of March 25th, 1947, commented "It is a particular source of gratification that each local authority will be obliged to appoint a children's officer. The work of securing for deprived children a normal home life is essentially personal and the Children's Officer will be the key person."

Mr Chuter Ede, the Home Secretary, in guiding the Children Bill through its final stages, told Parliament that "in the future much happiness would be created and many promising lives preserved through the skill, affection and attention of those officers."[9] Children's officers were to be supported in their departments by trained staff, both in field social work and in residential Homes. The fact that "large sections of the staff caring for ... children were without any special training for the task" in the Curtis Committee's opinion had been "in part responsible for unsatisfactory standards where these existed."[10] A Central Training Council, as recommended by the Committee, was set up in 1947 and several training courses were established before the Children Act, 1948 placed most of the Committee's recommendations on the statute book.

The Children Act was warmly supported by government and opposition alike. It was part of the post-war determination to bring about necessary changes and its implementation commenced at a time of optimism and enthusiasm for social improvements of many kinds. The first children's officers undertook their task with pioneering zeal. A number of them were women, a new phenomenon in British local government. Most were chief officers heading departments and directly responsible to a statutorily appointed children's committee, but the expectations of the Curtis Committee, local authorities, and the children's officers themselves were that they would be personally involved with children in care, their parents, relatives and friends and the staff and agencies directly concerned with providing services. Initially only a minority of children's departments were too large for this to be wholly impracticable, but rapid growth and further legislation soon made these early expectations less realistic. Nevertheless, by comparison with social services departments, particularly since 1974, even most large children's departments were small and relatively intimate and senior staff, including the chief officer, were often closely in touch with a range of people and detail now rarely, if ever, likely to be seen by top management.

Practice and policy in children's departments varied greatly from the outset. This was clearly shown in a study of fifty local authority child care services carried out in the early

1960s.[11] After examining many aspects of them and their relationships with other relevant statutory and voluntary services, the study concluded that there was much evidence to suggest that a standard child care service did not exist. Wide variations were found in the relative numbers of field staff employed, in the qualifications they possessed and in the number and kind of institutions which the different children's departments maintained. "Differences in attitude made themselves felt in the amount of emphasis that was placed upon ... the parental rights and duties and the prime importance of the natural family on the one hand, and on the protection for the child in the face of inadequate and harmful home circumstances, on the other."[12] Differences were also seen to exist in policies and practice related, for example, to family emergencies such as mothers' short-term illnesses and confinements, to delinquent children, juvenile court work, and illegitimate children. Further differences existed in practice concerning discharges from care, the use of various legal constraints and powers, methods of substitute care, and preventive work directed towards maintaining children in their own homes and avoiding their appearance before juvenile courts. Local traditions, historical accident, political influences, personality factors and many social differences played their part in producing the variations discovered.

The local authority responsible for the care of the people about whom this book is written was one of the fifty in the study. It was described as having a tendency to provide care for all the deprived children in its area rather than to spread the task amongst voluntary organizations and other services. It also received young offenders on fit person orders in preference to their committal to approved schools and it met a higher than average proportion of the total need problem within its boundaries. The proportion of residential accommodation provided was low in relation to numbers in care, though higher than average long-term care problems were dealt with as well as relatively high proportions of short-term emergencies. There was a tendency to retain fit person

orders in force longer than average and the overall policy of
the child care service was described as being "liberal" or
"protective".

The area in which the service was provided was described
as having an unplanned population increase of which a large
number were newcomers, combined with underdeveloped
services for the homeless and lower than average expenditure
on a number of services complementary to the child care
service, including home-helps and day nurseries. Between
1948 and 1970 the local authority was served by two
children's officers, one from 1948 to 1950 and the other from
1951 to 1970. During that time many changes took place in
child care services, nationally and locally. Further legislation
after 1948 increased local authority responsibilities to
children and young persons[13] and additional work stemming
from the legislation, growing public expectations and rising
standards of professional practice led to substantial increases
in field and residential staff and in administrative and office
support for them. National and local training facilities
increased and methods of work changed and developed.

In general, "legislation and practice (the latter often far in
advance of the former) moved from a narrow concern with
the provision of good substitute care for deprived children to
a much broader commitment to prevention of deprivation
and delinquency, to work with the whole family and to care
for the delinquent as well as the deprived child."[14]

The children's department in question developed over the
years from a totally unqualified service in 1948 to one in
which, by 1970, over 90% of its field social workers and 50%
of its residential staff were professionally qualified. These
staff provided practical work training facilities for sixty or
more professional social work students each year. (The two
professional colleagues who were involved with the children's
officer in the discussions recorded in this book were both
training officers in the department.) Some examples of the
changes which took place and the policy and practice of the
department have been described in a further research study

carried out shortly after the social services department took the place of the former specialized services.[15] Using written records made at the time of the events and policies described, the research examined some of the main characteristics of the child care service from 1948, when it inherited the former public assistance institutions, to 1970, the last year of the specialized service. It describes how a number of the old institutions were closed and new properties purchased or built. These were not very small children's Homes, as recommended by the Curtis Committee, but buildings which were able to accommodate twenty to thirty children in small "family groups", living in their own special rooms with their own special staff attached. The department was "hesitant to commit itself to the Curtis model, seeing the difficulties in placing some large families together in the smaller homes, and anticipating greater staffing difficulties. The small size of family group homes made it difficult to pay high enough salaries to attract qualified staff ... and where the burden of care rested on only two or three people, turnover could result in considerable disruption for the children." One nursery was retained "for the handicapped, damaged or those who had already suffered foster home breakdowns. It (the department) sought to avoid further damage by, amongst other things, "vertical" family grouping (covering all ages), high staff ratios, continuity of staff, extensive and reliable outside contacts." Fostering was developed by the appointment of additional social workers from the early 1950s onwards, and a policy of personalizing the service was pursued in a variety of ways. One small example was a decision at the end of 1951, when it was "resolved that foster children (as well as children in homes) should receive gifts together with letters from their officer and the committee, in place of the postal orders of the past."[16]

Preventive and rehabilitative work with families in their own homes began in 1952 when a special worker was appointed. "The appointment was the first of its kind in the child care service."[17] Other features of the department described in the study included the establishment of a panel method for decision making in adoption and fostering, the setting up of a regional adoption group, consultation with foster parents, a policy of consultation with residential staff and parity of residential with field social workers, support to voluntary agencies and the appointment of a specialist officer to advise staff and clients on welfare rights and benefits. The department as a whole was described as being organized on the basis that continuity of relationship between child, family and social worker (field or residential) was important and that field social workers "followed" their children wherever they were, inside or outside the county's boundaries.[18]

The practice, of which these and other examples are described in the research study, was shaped by a variety of influences including the findings of the Curtis Committee, practice guidance as taught to professional students on their qualifying courses, the interpretations of official policy given by Home Office Children's Department Inspectors, and research and practice of child care as expounded by writers such as Bowlby, Winnicott, Wills and Lyward amongst others. In some areas of practice the department gained much from the experiences of voluntary organizations such as the Family Service Units, and from other professional disciplines such as psychiatry, paediatrics and psychology working together on practical day-to-day problems. In addition the cumulative experience of the child care service itself, especially when recorded, discussed, collated and analysed, formed a growing source of knowledge to assist in developing policy and skill. In this experience, for those who were ready to listen and learn, the children themselves had much to offer, more perhaps than could be learned from any other source. Many people who worked in the department deeply valued their opportunities for first-hand experience and learning in this way and were also prepared, when possible, to involve the children's officer in personal contacts with the children. One way of doing this was a practice of arranging for children and the children's officer to meet when the children and their social workers were at the headquarters office or passing through. Sometimes these encounters were very brief, an exchange of greetings, a friendly chat and a cup of tea; sometimes they were much more, depending on time and circumstances. Combined with visits to children's Homes, some foster homes and a variety of other contacts, these meeting points enabled a substantial number of children in care to be known by and to know the children's officer as well as other staff.

It was also considered important to try to obtain, from time to time, first-hand knowledge of how the children felt about the services they received from the department. An attempt to do this was made by inviting some of those who were almost eighteen years of age to see the children's officer before they went out of care. Over the years, a number accepted the invitation and the discussions which took place were often illuminating and rewarding. The boys and girls came sometimes with their social workers, sometimes alone. Sometimes the purpose of the visit was already known, sometimes it was unexpected, but in either case it was made explicit that the comments of those who had been experiencing the services would be helpful in enabling those providing them to be more sensitive to other children's needs in the future.

Responses varied, but quite a number of young people were able to use the opportunity to talk about their time "in care" and about what they thought had helped them most, as well as what they had resented or not understood. Most of them gave the impression of being glad to be invited to say what they thought even if they were not always able to make full use of the opportunity. Occasionally the response came much later as when a woman of twenty-three wrote and said, "The worst thing you did, you didn't do anything bad, except that you stopped being involved with me after I was eighteen."

By 1969 the child care service had been in existence for twenty-one years. The fact that by this time many people employed in it were pressing for further reorganization of personal social services, along the lines recommended by the Seebohm Committee, did not detract from their sense of the importance of what had been achieved in the previous twenty years. In the local authority in question the idea arose of reviewing the children's department's development at its "coming of age". This led to a day of activities in July 1969 to which former committee members and staff were invited by the current committee and staff. In order to involve some of those who had received the service it was decided to invite one person who had gone out of care at eighteen years old in each year between 1948 and 1969. A number of people who had remained in care until they were eighteen were still in touch with members of the department, partly as the result of a practice initiated some years earlier of sending a Christmas letter and card each year to all those whose whereabouts were still known, and partly because the department's policy was to continue to offer assistance, advice and contact as long as these were found helpful to the people concerned.

The review day's proceedings included visits to various residential establishments, an exhibition of photographs of children and staff over the years and a programme of comment and reminiscences by men and women who had participated as staff and elected members in the events and developments of the service between 1948 and 1969. Letters and tape recordings were received from a number of former staff who had gone abroad and many others made long journeys from various parts of the country to attend. Several of the men and women who were invited because they had remained in care until they were eighteen found the experience stimulating and enjoyable and sought an opportunity to talk to the children's officer about it afterwards. During this discussion the children's officer asked for their views on whether they, and perhaps others, might be willing to discuss their own experience and feelings about being in care in greater depth than had been possible before, and with the purpose of enabling the service to learn by their experience. They welcomed the idea and thought that others might too. Later several others were approached or volunteered as a result of the Christmas letter in 1969 which explained that a small consumer reaction study was being considered. From this beginning the group of ten people whose discussions provided the material for this book was formed.

2   The Group

The ten people who met the children's officer and her two colleagues to discuss their experiences in care had either responded to invitations following their involvement in the children's department review day in 1969 or had expressed an interest in the children's officer's proposal to form a small consumer group, outlined in her 1969 Christmas letter to them. Their selection was partly related to local availability (though one member travelled a long distance to meetings) and partly to the spread of experience they represented and the different periods in which they had received care during the life of the child care service. The most important considerations, however, were their willingness to participate and their concern for the purpose of the group. During the course of the meetings three other people, all young men, came on one occasion each. They made some brief but clear contributions, but for individual reasons did not attend again. What they said has been incorporated in the accounts of group discussions, but because they were not regular members they have not been identified by name nor has any information been given about them. The ten regular members were not able to come to every meeting, but when they were absent this was usually due to their own or their children's illnesses, previously planned holidays, inability on some occasions to have time off from work or obtain baby sitting service or to some other serious reason. Their general approach to the meetings of the group was to give them as much priority as their personal circumstances allowed and most went to considerable trouble to ensure that they could attend whenever possible.

The first meeting took place at ten o'clock on a Saturday morning in March 1970 in the children's officer's office. This room was large and comfortably furnished and after coffee and biscuits on arrival, the group sat down in a circle of armchairs. A low table with a tape recorder on it stood at one side. After a general welcome the children's officer began the meeting by explaining that its purpose was to examine her proposal to form a small consumer group. If at the end of the meeting the proposal was not supported, there would be no more meetings and no record of the discussion would be kept. If after discussion, however, it was decided to set up a group and hold a series of meetings, a tape recording from the outset would ensure that nothing was lost and that those who would otherwise have to take notes could give their full attention to the group's discussion. It was readily agreed that a recording of this first meeting should be made and from this point the table with the tape recorder on it was moved into the centre of the circle. It remained there at all future meetings and from the beginning did not appear to inhibit discussion in any way.

The children's officer then went on to rehearse in detail the purpose of the group, how the proposal had arisen and how the membership of the group had come about. She explained that because of the way in which members had been invited or had volunteered and the size of the group, it could not be regarded as representative of others who had not expressed an interest or who might have felt too negative about an invitation to respond to it. Nevertheless, she suggested that this did not prevent the purpose of the proposal being achieved, that is, to gain some knowledge of consumers' views and feelings about the child care service in order to try to increase its sensitivity to individual need.

All members of the group were then invited to introduce themselves by giving their name and a little general information about themselves. The children's officer and her two colleagues joined in and everyone contributed briefly details of where they lived, their job, their immediate family and how they had either entered public care as a child or become involved in the service which provided it, as an adult. These introductions over, the group moved on to consider some of the practical issues in which their experience might be of value, issues like the staffing of children's Homes, relationships between children and their social workers and the selection of foster homes for children in care. The morning passed quickly and easily and by lunchtime everyone was talking freely and candidly. The arrangements for the first meeting had included an invitation to have lunch together and continue discussion afterwards until 2.30 in the afternoon. A home-cooked buffet lunch was provided in an adjacent room and then the group returned with coffee for the remainder of the meeting.

During the morning discussion members of the group had begun to describe some of their own experiences. It was clear that their memories were fresh and vivid to them although, through the passage of time, they were able to be more reflective than would have been possible when the events they recalled were happening. Some had also gained fresh perspectives through the eyes of marriage partners or as parents themselves. Informal discussion had continued over lunch and by the beginning of the shorter afternoon session, there was no doubt that the group wished to continue to meet. They believed they might contribute something of value which could be used by the professional workers, and welcomed the opportunity to do so. One or two made it clear, in addition, that the discussions might help them to sort out residual feelings and gain a better understanding of the earlier parts of their lives. Some expressed the hope that they might have additional information about themselves. These reactions had been anticipated by the children's officer and her colleagues and they responded by offering private time for discussion with any member of the group who wished to have it. At various times during the months that followed five of the group took this opportunity to talk over and clarify some of the facts, impressions and feelings about their lives which still troubled them.

Agreement having been reached to establish a group, the children's officer then invited suggestions of topics for discussion. These were not slow in coming. Amongst the most immediate were the need for children to have information about their own backgrounds; contact with parents; being moved about; foster parents; favouritism in groups; school and religious education; the development of individual personality and interests; alienation; work and the adolescent. As one member of the group put it, "That'll keep us going until next year, won't it?" It was agreed that these topics could act as starting points for discussion, which would develop as the group learned to work together. Finally a series of dates for future meetings were sorted out, allowance being made for known commitments such as holidays which had already been booked. It was decided that the pattern of the first meeting was the most convenient that could be arranged and all subsequent meetings, of which there were ten, took place on Saturdays from 10.0 in the morning to about 2.30 in the afternoon. Coffee and biscuits made a welcoming start and a late "breakfast" for some who had difficult travelling or home arrangements, everyone shared a home-cooked buffet lunch at 12.30 and a final cup of tea before leaving. Meetings were spread out at approximately monthly intervals, the last taking place in December, 1970.

Before the first meeting ended the children's officer shared with the group her hope that, in addition to any immediate use which she and her colleagues might make of the material from the discussions, she might write a book incorporating it for use in a wider context. There was considerable support for this and at the last meeting of the group, as well as on other occasions, members mentioned this long-term objective and made inquiries about its progress. They knew that their identity would not be revealed but they were happy that their experiences, feelings and comment should be used.

The members of the group which was thus formed will be called Alex, Andrew, Anne, Barry, Carol, Derek, Margaret, Martin, Miranda and Valerie. These are not their real names and the information about them which follows has been disguised where it might have revealed their identity. Their ages relate to 1970 and are approximate.

ALEX, aged nineteen, had been received into care when he was nine years old because his parents separated after a very stormy period. His father was a skilled technician who was keen for his son to have a good education. Alex first went to an observation and assessment centre from which, for a time, he attended a local grammar school. This was not a successful arrangement and he was later placed in a large residential community during term time but spent all his holidays with his father who was devoted to him. After leaving school Alex was employed for a time as a residential social worker. During the course of the group meetings he had an illness which lasted for several months.

ANDREW, aged thirty-four, was one of a family of brothers who were all received into care before 1948 when their home broke up because their father was serving overseas and their mother became ill. They were placed in an isolated and institutional children's Home where Andrew was unhappy. This Home was subsequently closed and the children transferred to another where he was much happier.

On leaving school he became a boy entrant in one of the armed forces. This proved unsuitable and he obtained his discharge within a year. He could not return to the second children's Home but was found lodgings with an elderly woman. During this time a family nearby befriended him and, when an older child left home, they invited Andrew to live with them and gradually became like a family to him.

He married shortly after completing his national service and by 1970 had three sons, the eldest of whom had gained entry to a grammar school. Andrew was a local councillor, earned his living as a salesman, and was buying his own house.

ANNE, aged twenty, was the oldest of a family of three. Her mother suddenly left her and the other children when Anne was eight, taking with her most of Anne's knowledge of her early life. She could remember very little except moving about a great deal. The family was living on a farm when her mother's second marriage began to go wrong. When she left there was no trace of where she had gone and she never came back. Anne's stepfather could not care for them and the children were all received into care for a time. Later he removed the youngest child, born of the second marriage, and it was years before Anne and her brother saw their little sister again.

The two children were placed in a small children's Home where after a time Anne became very attached to the married couple in charge. However, after many discussions and much anxious thought, it was decided to try to find the children a permanent foster home. Anne did not want to leave the children's Home but believed her brother would benefit from being fostered.

Eventually they were placed and for the next few years travelled with their foster parents wherever their foster father's career took them. Part of the time they were abroad where a voluntary organization undertook supervision on behalf of the local authority. When they returned to England it was clear that all was not well and after a time the foster parents asked for Anne's removal. Later they also parted from Anne's brother.

Anne became pregnant while still unmarried and later allowed her baby to be placed for adoption.

BARRY, aged twenty-eight, was one of several brothers whose mother died and whose father was unable to care for them by himself. They were received into care when Barry was eight and placed all together in an observation and assessment centre, from which they later went to a group of children's Homes. During their time there the eldest brother reached school leaving age and went to work elsewhere. The boys' father visited them in the Homes and they also went out to visit relatives.

When Barry was about twelve, he was boarded out and later went to a college of further education where he learned a skilled craft in which he was subsequently employed. His foster home remained his family base until he married and found a house in a nearby village. By his mid-twenties he had become a valued member of the community in which he lived and was involved in organizing youth work in his spare time.

CAROL, aged twenty, was the child of an unmarried mother who could not care for her but who also found it difficult to let her go to someone else. She visited Carol from time to time at the residential nursery where she spent her first few years but it eventually became clear that she would never be able to provide a home for her. Carol was placed with long-term foster parents who later adopted her, but continued to foster other children. Most of these were short-stay, but some stayed and became long-stay foster children. All these were boys. Carol found the coming and going disturbing and was sometimes threatened with removal by her adoptive mother as a means of disciplining her behaviour. Their relationship deteriorated during adolescence and by the time Carol left school it was necessary for the local authority to receive her back into care as a preventive measure to avoid a total breakdown of the family bonds. She lived for various periods in a voluntary hostel, in lodgings, and in a local authority hostel. Meanwhile she trained for a career in the hotel trade. She met her husband when she about nineteen and later married from her adoptive parents' home. Their wedding reception was held in the village where she had grown up and was a traditional family occasion.

DEREK, aged twenty-two, was removed from the care of his parents with his younger sister on the grounds of neglect when they were both tiny children. Their mother, who was very young, was sent to a rehabilitation centre for neglectful parents but when she returned she and her husband became homeless. They drifted apart and the children never saw them again.

Derek and his sister, Linda, lived together for a time in a children's Home while the possibility of boarding them out together was explored. They were both introduced to several couples and spent trial visits and weekends with them. Each time the prospective foster parents found Derek easy to relate to but not Linda who was fretful and miserable, though very pretty. Eventually it was decided to place Derek in a foster home and leave Linda in the children's Home. In this foster home Derek was brought up to believe that he was adopted, although social workers continued to visit. The foster parents had a son of their own who accepted him as a brother and in later years, when first the foster father and then the foster mother died, the two young men continued to live together in the family home. Linda's life meanwhile had been very unhappy and when the brother and sister were re-introduced in their late adolescence, Derek found she had many serious problems.

MARGARET, aged twenty-six, knew nothing about her natural parents except that her mother had been about sixteen when she was born and that she had been persuaded by her own mother to allow Margaret to be adopted. She had been chosen by her adoptive parents from amongst a number of other babies at a convent home in Canada.

The family had returned to England when Margaret was about seven and after a series of family and housing upheavals, her father was found to have a serious health condition for which there was no cure. Margaret was in care briefly during this time while her mother was in a mental hospital. Later when she was about twelve, the family moved again, became homeless and Margaret was received into care once more. After a period in an observation and assessment centre she was placed in the same group of Homes as Barry. Later she was boarded out with a single woman who also cared for handicapped children, some of whom were there at the same time as Margaret. She was not happy in this foster home and became even more unhappy when her father died.

After she left school she was trained in dressmaking and

later as a nursery nurse. In her late teens she met the father of her two children. They later separated and she set up house on her own in a caravan with the children. She did voluntary work at a nearby hospital and occasionally worked as a home-help.

MARTIN, aged twenty-three, was the baby of a large family. When they were all received into care the other children remained together in a children's Home until they were fostered in pairs, but Martin was placed in a long-stay foster home at six months old with a childless couple who wanted to make him a member of their family on a permanent basis. Their relatives and friends supported them in this and the placement became a *de facto* adoption though its status was based on a fostering agreement.

As a growing boy Martin developed a love for the country and a local farmer took him under his wing and offered him adult friendship and interest. In consequence when he left school he decided to go on the land.

MIRANDA, aged twenty, had parents who had both suffered parental deprivation in their own childhoods. By the time she was born their marriage was at the point of breakdown and she was received into care at a few days old. She spent her first two to three years in a residential nursery because her parents' attitudes made fostering impracticable. They then decided to try living together again and removed her from care to live with them. In a short time the experiment failed and she was placed privately by her parents in three foster homes in the course of nine to twelve months. Neighbours' complaints that the child was suffering brought her to the local authority's notice again and she was received into care. She was placed in a very stable children's Home where there were qualified staff who intended to stay for some years. Miranda became very attached to them. Her parents' continued marital strife eventually ended in divorce and care and control of Miranda was given to the local authority.

During adolescence Miranda's difficulties became more

than the local school could accommodate and she was placed in a boarding school, returning each holiday to the same children's Home and the staff she knew. She did not like the boarding school which experienced unexpected difficulties while she was there and closed for a time. Almost at school leaving age she returned to the children's Home.

She was happy to be back and later moved out to lodgings not far away where she began to develop into a very capable young woman. When she sought permission to work with a family in France this was given and she found the experience very helpful. By the time the group meetings began, she had taken secretarial training and acquired a good post and was living in her own small flat. She undertook a considerable journey from where she lived to attend the group meetings.

VALERIE, aged twenty-two, appeared when she was a teenager before a juvenile court with a younger brother, charged with stealing. Before the court hearing the two children were placed in an observation and assessment centre, Valerie believing that they would both go home afterwards. It was a shock to her when her mother told the magistrates she could not control her and did not want her at home again. She was committed to the care of the local authority and for various reasons, inlcuding nearness to home and the fact that she was doing well at school, remained at the observation and assessment centre until she reached school leaving age.

She then went to live at a girls' hostel where work was readily available locally, where she was still near to home and where the staff were accustomed to helping adolescents with their problems. Valerie had continued to steal whilst in care and eventually in-patient psychiatric help was sought. The treatment she received was completely successful and Valerie gained considerable insight and understanding of herself and her relationships with her family. When she left hospital, after a short return to the hostel, she shared a flat with another adolescent girl in care. Soon afterwards she met and married her husband and by 1970 had two sons, one still only a small baby.

3   Family Ties

Amongst the topics proposed by group members for discussion were the need for children in care to have information about their own backgrounds and their contacts with parents. These broad outlines encompassed issues and feelings which were basic to the whole experience of being in care and formed part of the background to the group's discussions throughout. This chapter, therefore, only begins to explore group members' perceptions of family ties and relationships which are further discussed and illuminated in more detail in later chapters.

Families and what they mean to individuals, not only as children but also in adult life, were of great significance to all the members of the group, whether their families were related by blood ties, by remarriage, by adoption or by fostering. Like many other people whose family backgrounds have not been disrupted or permanently lost, they had both positive and negative feelings about them. Their experiences of natural parents had varied greatly. Margaret, Carol and Martin had all been received into care as babies; they had few or no conscious memories of their mothers and also knew very little about them or their fathers. Andrew and Derek had lived with their parents when they were babies and toddlers, perhaps longer in Andrew's case, but they remembered very little. Barry's mother had died when he was about eight but he was still in regular touch with his father for several years after that until he too died. Alex' and Miranda's parents were both alive, but presenting problems for them except for Alex' father who was helpful and supportive to him. Valerie had strong feelings of rejection by her mother, and her own father, whom she did not remember, had been replaced by a stepfather. Anne, who had been deserted at eight years old, did not appear to remember her natural father and was still grieving and searching for her mother twelve years later. Such experience could not provide a balanced view of natural parenthood since even when relationships were established and loving some had been cut off by death. Even in happier circumstances children's perceptions of the reasons for family events and decisions are likely to be coloured by their limited understanding, their dependence and their fears of change and loss. Lack of experience also makes comparisons with other families difficult at the time and it is often only in retrospect that the picture may look clearer. It was evident in discussion that this was the experience of some of the group.

Their general view, based on their own and other children's experiences, was that some parents are basically inadequate, and unable to offer the care, support and encouragement which group members who were parents were trying to give their own children. On the other hand they knew only too well how much most children want and need their own parents, however inadequate they may seem to be. A frequent and practical reminder of this conflict was visiting day in children's Homes. The children's officer had recalled a boy she had known whose mother had been a very disturbed personality. She constantly promised him she would visit him and then failed to come.

"He would go almost frantic on the Saturday afternoon, waiting for her, but she seldom came. His way of working it out of his system was to run frantically round and round the house outside, trying to get rid of this awful feeling of disappointment and frustration because nobody had come." Barry remembered many such occasions "where boys were expecting parents to come on the Saturday afternoon, and as soon as they knew during the week, they'd be saying "My mum's coming to see me on Saturday" — and perhaps they didn't turn up. I remember it used to create a terrible scene.

They built themselves up so much that the parents were coming to see them.''

Margaret did not want her adoptive mother to come and see her; on the other hand, she recalled that when parents did come in some families ''there were scenes and upsets'' and the children ''used to cringe terribly. Some of them used to hide, like Eric when his father was coming to see him. We used to have to look for Eric when his father was coming, and we'd find him in the most strange places, at the bottom of the garden, or in the field next door.''

When Eric and his sisters were discharged from care and went home again, Margaret, who had been friendly with one of the sisters, had heard that their father ''was married to another woman and this upset the whole family . . . the whole family hated it. I don't really know what happened after that but in the children's Home they hated their parents coming as much as I hated my mother coming and yet there were other children who desperately wanted their parents. I can remember the big gap between those who didn't and those who did.''

Sometimes the children's longings for their parents to be more adequate, more like other people, lay behind their rejection of them. They were acutely embarrassed when they needed to feel supported and pleased to belong to their parents. ''I can remember my mother trying to gas herself when I was a child and doing things I thought not proper; mothers don't do things like this. I withdrew from her to the point where I thought 'I don't want to associate myself with you because you are doing things that aren't right.' She embarrassed me and I think the fact that she couldn't cope when Daddy died and when Daddy was very ill, she just couldn't cope; I had so many friends at school whose mothers were on their own and yet they managed to cope.''

Four of the group had experience of step-parents. In the main this had not been happy.

''My mother remarried about, how many years ago, about twelve isn't it?'' Miranda recalled. ''And I see him, I don't

even call him stepfather, just my mother's husband. I have
known him for years but I don't really know him at all. I just
know he is a crafty old thing. My real father, he remarried I
think about five or six years ago? And from the word go his
wife didn't want to know anything about me, she just didn't
want to know. I was at boarding school at the time and he
visited me and he brought this strange woman and we went
out for a drive. Then he came again about a month later and
said 'Do you like Auntie June?' as she was then called — I
said 'Yes, she's all right.' I was about fourteen then and he
said 'Well, I'm going to marry her.' I said 'Oh, are you, can I
come to the wedding?' and they were married down on
the south coast which was about three hundred miles from
my boarding school. I had the weekend off from the
boarding school and I went to the wedding and I think from
the actual wedding reception, after they were legally married,
she just didn't want to know. I went to stay one Christmas
and do you know, it was terrible. I went the day before
Christmas and I was back on Boxing Day. I haven't seen her
since that day.''

''We had three or four moves before we met up with my
stepfather,'' said Anne. ''I can remember being introduced
to him and thinking he's horrible, and hiding behind Mum's
skirts. One of the first few things he said to me was 'Ah, so
you're Anne, you're my little girl now.' I hated that, it took
me ages to get used to him after that. He was a farm hand. He
got this job on a farm and things started to go wrong and
when my mother left us, I came into care. I think he was quite
fond of us, you know. I can remember the day that the police
came to the house to see about us kids and I remember he was
sitting on the sofa and he was crying, not sobbing, just sort of
weeping, and I thought 'Oh, I didn't think you cared for us'
and then these tears — I don't know if they were crocodile
tears or not. I was quite touched at that, you know, it really
stuck in my mind.''

Even when a step-parent had seemed like a natural parent
anxiety was created by learning the truth in a distressing way.

Valerie told the group, "I didn't know my real father and the person I called Dad, I didn't know he wasn't my father until just before I came into care, a few days before, and then I overheard it accidentally when my mother was talking to a policeman you see, and of course I just didn't know what to believe. I didn't know where to go and then I came into care as I said, and I was quite happy at first, but after that I didn't want to stay."

Gaps in knowledge and gaps in relationships were both problems for members of the group. It can be difficult to know how to relate to parents who have not been part of a shared life in childhood. Other people's assumptions about families and family relationships may not take account of these difficulties.

Andrew described his experience and how he dealt with it. "I was in a bit of a dilemma about five or six years ago, when a policeman was on my doorstep and he said 'Mr Smith,' and I said, 'Yes.' 'Well, I've come to inform you that your mother is seriously ill in hospital.' I just stood there dumbfounded, you know, and I said 'Well, what am I to do? I've never seen her,' and he said 'Well, I have done my duty, I've given you the message' and rumbled off. I could see the look on his face, obviously he thought 'Well, it's your mother, you know, if you haven't got any care for your mother, my God, you must be a right one, you know.' And of course I didn't have a chance to explain to him or anything, that I didn't even know her. I remember picking up the 'phone and contacting my brother and saying 'Well, what shall we do? Did we ought to go in and see her?' Any other person with a natural parental background would have gone in straight away but we didn't. We decided against it after so long and not having any contact, that we didn't want to start anything up that possibly we wouldn't be able to control and possibly we wouldn't like."

Relationships with brothers and sisters can also become more difficult and complicated because of experiences whilst in care and because of what members of the group described as being "split up quite a lot." By the early 1950s considerable efforts were being made to keep brothers and sisters together but nevertheless they often became separated and in Andrew's experience, much of which preceded the setting up of children's departments, his separation from his brothers had had long-term consequences.

"I don't get on particularly well with my younger brother now. I never see him. As a matter of fact he was in trouble. I had just got married and somebody came knocking on my door saying he was in trouble, that he had given my name as one of his relations and could I help him any way, and I remember I journeyed all the way to London and he lived with us for a time. Even then I didn't get on very well with him, he seemed to be very rebellious. I even fixed him up for a job. He was very hard to handle and as a matter of fact, when I went and fetched him from London, even though I was mature then, I was rather frightened of him. He struck me as one of those chaps who would fly off the deep end and do something drastic, a highly dangerous type to have around. He gave me a very worrying time and in the end he did up and leave and I've lost contact with him again. I think possibly if we had all been together things at later stages of life might have been different, even for him although he is my brother and very unstable, I think possibly being a bit closer it could have turned out differently. There could perhaps have been more contact between us after we left the Home."

Anne and her brother were inseparable when they were young and were boarded out together. Only later did it become clear that the foster parents took Anne because they wanted her brother. Eventually the foster home rejected them both, first Anne and later her brother. Both children had been through experiences of loss and disappointment in the foster home and their own relationship suffered. "In the end we were apart. We are very apart now, my brother and me. There's a sort of, I don't know, a very wide gap between us." At the time of the group meetings Anne was expecting a baby by a man to whom she was not married. Asked whether she thought she and her brother would move together again as they got older she said, "It sounds an awful thing to say but I've given him up as a brother. As an acquaintance, well, we keep in touch; as a brother I don't think he'll ever be a brother to me. He definitely needs somebody though. He's very cold and aggressive. When he found out I was pregnant, I told him, when it was physically obvious you know, he was violently angry, he was in a rage, he started poking me about, and, from my own brother, I thought 'Well, OK, you've more right than anybody else to do this, but you've still no right to do this' and I was quite shocked. I thought, 'If anybody would understand, you would, our own mother did this years ago.' I thought he would understand. He's so bitter inside. I suppose I'm a big soft-hearted thing, but he's exactly the opposite. He wouldn't help anybody, he'd say 'You're in that trouble, you get yourself out of it, I've got my own troubles.' He's very self-centred." Asked whether she thought he might change if he had children of his own, she said, "It would probably be the making of him. I think he really needs somebody that much. Now he is becoming accustomed to the fact that I'm going to have a baby one of the last things he said to me before I left Scotland was 'Hey, I'm going to be an uncle now!' It just sort of struck him. I think that endeared him to me more than anything else."

The experience of being separated from their family must produce anxiety, fear and a degree of shock in most children even if the preparation for it has been careful and reassuring. For some it is accompanied by additional pain because of the lack of preparation and because of what it reveals about family relationships. Valerie described to the group how she was committed to care on a fit person order, and what she had to face in consequence; "Oh gosh, it was horrible. I felt awful. The chap on the bench, he was very nice, he told me not to be frightened or anything but it was all those people, there were so many people there. It scared me to death. I wasn't really sure [what was happening] because when I was taken home by the police' the night before, my Mum was there but my Dad wasn't there, he was at work. My brother and I, as I said, were both taken home and then the policewoman said did my Mum want to look after us, so she said 'Yes', but a few hours later she took me back down to the police station and I spent the night there. And to go to court from the police station, well I'd never want to go through it again!"

Someone asked her where she slept at the police station. "In a cell. They had a woman police officer there. Oh, she was nice enough, but I didn't think it was fair that my Mum had kept my brother and sent me off. She just said I was the worst of the two and it was all my fault."

"I went in a police car to the court and it just scared me to death. I didn't know what was happening. I didn't know what to expect. The thing that frightened me most of all was the people, so many people, and so many pieces of paper. My mother was in court; I hated her. Well she stood in court and she said that I was wicked and she could not look after me any more, that I was out of control, and of course my Dad wasn't there, he couldn't go, and if he'd been there I think he'd have stood up for me you know. I think it was only because I didn't get on with my Mum that she did it; more or less for spite perhaps. If I was [out of control] it wasn't my fault because she used to go out to work at night and me being the eldest, I was expected to look after the younger children while she went to work."

Fortunately Valerie was able to share her painful memories with her husband. "He just said, 'What's happened has happened, that's all there is to it." He's that kind of person. It doesn't bother him at all. He said, "If you want to go to the meetings, go, it's your life. You do what you want."' She was able to talk to him about the meetings because he was "quite interested".

Some members of the group felt parents were often evasive and tended to see events and problems more from their own point of view than they should. They put themselves in a good light, sometimes to the detriment of the children who depended on them, and on occasions were prepared to protect themselves at the expense of truth. Margaret recounted how she and her mother had recently been reminiscing. "She said I was about eight when I first asked 'Where did I come from? What time of day was I born?' and she couldn't tell me; but she didn't tell me why she couldn't tell me until I was older. I was going into care and until then I didn't find out I was adopted, but if I'd known then when I asked that question it would have been easier to accept. 'Oh well, you're adopted so therefore I can't tell you what time you were born, but it doesn't really matter, it's just one of those things,' would have been a far better answer than 'Well, I've no idea, I can't remember.' "

Valerie had met the same problem even more unsuccessfully. "I always used to ask her [mother] who was my father and even now I still don't know and not even my gran will tell me and she [mother] just didn't seem interested enough to tell me anything."

Miranda said her parents "were not prepared to tell me the truth and I still don't know." She saw her father as lacking in proper courage to defend her when she needed it: "My father is obviously not the man I thought he was. I mean he is not a man, he's a mouse. He just hasn't got the guts to stand up and say [to his second wife] that 'She's my daughter, I married you and you're going to have to put up with it. She's not that bad, I am sure you could.' "

Miranda's experience made her feel that parents were so self-interested that some outside person was needed who, because they were independent, could take a more objective view of a family's problems. "I think parents try to bring themselves out in a good light; hide all the bad things and put in all the good ones."

"You hear different sides of the story from each party. You've got to have an independent person that can put the final lid on the whole thing. Say when a family splits up, mother goes one way, father goes the other, and the children go into a Home, then that third person is *the* important person to put the final touch to it because the mother will blame the father and vice versa.''

Carol had much less confidence that a third person from outside the family could really get at the reality of a situation.

''Somebody coming from the outside can't really tell your proper position here, if you know what I mean. My Mum and I were always rowing and sometimes I think she used to mention the rows to other people but she always put herself so that she had been in the right all the time. Yet to me, most of the time she had caused them or had said I couldn't have something, so really to me it was her fault. Yet she would always say that I had caused it.''

Andrew was inclined to agree with her and thought that social workers had difficulty in finding out the true facts of a situation. ''When a social worker is visiting someone, a family or something, I think they are liable to withhold some things. I don't think they are liable to come clean, as it were, completely.''

The experience of separation, even when it brought relief from other problems, as it did to Margaret, made a deep scar which gave continuing pain. ''I've got very divided loyalties about my mother.... When she says something about 'Oh, it's hard for you on your own with two children' I'll turn round and say 'Yes, well you got rid of me and there was only me' and I say it even now. I feel very bitter about it still.''

Yet Margaret could not bear other people to criticize her mother and as an adult had a continuing sense of responsibility for her — ''She tends to look up to me which I find frightening.''

Margaret felt everybody needed someone or something to cling to even if it were only to a memory. ''I've still got my father's camera . . . it's the only thing which I have literally hung on to.'' She loved her father ''desperately'' and after he died found it hard to relate closely to other people.

Although the majority of the group had had unsatisfactory experiences with natural parents when they were children, they showed a capacity to understand parents' difficulties, particularly since some were experiencing parenthood themselves. Personal stresses had already demonstrated how the breaking point is reached in some families, and though they were determined to avoid it at all costs, they were aware of how the pattern of deprivation can be repeated. Loneliness and the problems of bringing up a child without a second parent were hazards they recognized.

One member described how when she was first left alone, "I fought like anything to keep Christopher from going into a children's Home" but she wondered how she would have managed without the support of the children's department. Another member described how, when she was alone with her baby before she and the baby's father were married, she could not have coped "if he hadn't been interested. Even when I was pregnant he paid the rent on my flat for me, I didn't have to work." Other members, although they had not faced such problems themselves, thought "a second person there to visit regularly or be on hand in fairly close proximity" was essential. Loneliness is a terrible problem and "somebody to reassure you is important, to know that you are doing the right thing."

At such times "television is a great thing. You don't even need to listen to it but just to have a face in the room with you keeps you sane."

One of the men thought it might help "for a mother and child if you had a group of two or three together in a little block of flats, so that they could go along to the next-door neighbour and talk to them." One of the group who was a mother responded that that would be "fantastic" because "when the children are in bed and you can't go off, there are some nights when you think, "If only I could get out, if only I could go for a walk, if only I could do something." This is when you really need help, when you are on your own and the children in bed."

The loneliness and the pent-up frustration that can accompany it had reached a climax for Margaret since the previous meeting and she shared the experience with the group: "About a fortnight ago, I had just had enough and I took the children down to my mother and I said 'Mum, have the children for the night, I'm not going anywhere but I'm just fed up with the sole responsibility of them and the caravan and everything,' and I never realized that I had got to this point, I just didn't want to see the children. The next morning I did because I had had a break. But it is a horrible sensation when you just don't want to have anything to do with the responsibility of it. I suppose for some people it lasts a long time. I felt very guilty after I had said it, and I said 'Well, I don't really mean it,' but I did at that particular point."

Their own experiences as children appeared to be helping the group members who were parents to understand some of the needs of their own children. They were not only determined that they would bring them up themselves, but they were doing their best to provide what they saw as a good upbringing, making some demands but more appropriate ones, they felt, than those made on them as children. Andrew's surprise at how a boy in his own home had fared compared with a boy in a children's Home was expressed as follows:

"When I left the Home and went into lodgings I was rather surprised that the chap I was lodging with, the parents' son, he hadn't ever cleaned his shoes in his life. His parents had always cleaned his shoes and he was seventeen. I thought, 'My God, never cleaned his shoes, they always cleaned his shoes for him!' And I used to think, 'Well, I don't know, he's had it really easy,' you know."

Margaret had had experiences in a children's Home when cleaning shoes which she had resented and which she talked about on several occasions. She believed her children should help her but in ways which she thought helped them to feel they were sharing the tasks of a joint life rather than caring for themselves. "There are a few jobs I insist on. I know Christopher is only six, but I insist that he does help because I am on my own with the two children, but that is such as emptying the bins or putting out the milk bottles and things like this, but I wouldn't consider trying to make him make his own bed, or trying to get him cleaning his shoes and things like that because he doesn't need that sort of learning. He needs the learning of play and reading and anything that will better his mind; making a bed won't make him a better individual.''

Margaret shared with Andrew a concern for her children's education. Part of this undoubtedly stemmed from their own realization of the opportunities they had missed because they were in care and lacked the supportive interest of parents urging them to make progress and develop their innate potential.

"My children expect some form of encouragement," said Andrew. "They look forward to school open day and you inspecting their books, and looking through their desks and all their books, looking at the marks they get, looking at the reports they get at the end of term. Although they don't say so they seem to want you to make comments and I always make a point of making comments 'You are a bit low on so-and-so' and things like this. You point out the things that they ought to be aiming for. You are pushing them. This is something which I've done naturally and yet never had done for myself. I think it is so important. When my eldest who started grammar school last term, when he first asked if he could bring homework home we encouraged him. We were very pleased that he accepted that homework was the way to do extra study and get on. We encouraged him and made a point of trying to push, not hard, not to the extreme, but take an interest. Perhaps it's the natural inbred thing that you want to see your children get on.''

"This is what I felt that I lacked when I was in care and yet I never really thought about it other than I wanted to stay on at school and I wish there had been somebody there," Margaret responded. "Somebody there" meant somebody to persuade her to do more and to arrange for her to stay on at school, even though at the time she did not appear keen to do so. She described how she was trying to encourage her own children to do well. "I've said to Christopher 'Come on, try and do it! OK, you say it's a bit too hard but first show me that it's too hard and then I'll help you.' You try and be, if I say one step ahead of the child it sounds wrong, but you try and draw the child out instead of letting it go on as I felt I was let to go my own way."

In the first meeting of the group people had been talking together for less than an hour when the importance of this commitment of time and interest which loving parents expect to give their children became a theme in their discussion. "Every child yearns for individual attention" was the way Andrew put it. Such individual attention is difficult to achieve in group settings where members of staff may be required to try to relate to a number of children at the same time. Even in a family this can be difficult if the need of each individual is taken into account. Andrew's three boys were all at school. He said: "My youngest is five and they are all boys, but even now I can't give them the attention I would like to. It sometimes pricks my conscience and I sit and think I ought to have played with them a bit more or I ought to have done this with them and I haven't been able to, or I have spent a bit of extra time with the eldest who has just started grammar school going over his biology with him and have had to neglect the other two. I think it gets a bit hectic at that age, from about five years onwards. You've got to split so differently between the three; for instance with the eldest I'm talking about biology or reading his text book or something, and the other one perhaps having a game of conkers out in the yard or something, and the other one is just managing to read, so there are two or three different categories, you've got to devote your time on, to pay them equal attention."

The importance of families as a background for the security and development of individuals was something which for the members of the group had been emphasized by their own unsatisfactory experiences and loss. If children had to be in care they felt that in as many ways as possible the continuity and wholeness of their lives should be safeguarded, not only for their own sake, but for the sake of the family life they would later have themselves, with marriage partners and children of their own who would want to share their past as well as their present and future. "What was it like when you were in that Home, Dad?" Andrew's children had asked him. It would have been very important to him and to them if he had been able to tell them about their grandparents, perhaps their great-grandparents too.

4 Feeling "Different"

Although the feeling of being "different" as a result of needing to be in public care was not one of the group's first proposals for discussion, it emerged so often as one of their childhood problems that it seemed to merit a chapter of its own. It is well known that at least until late adolescence most children hate to feel different from their contemporaries and the groups with whom they are associating day by day. They put their parents under pressure to buy clothing and equipment, to agree to certain bedtimes and activities because "everybody has one" or "everyone else does, so why can't I?" They hate to think that they stand out in some embarrassing way from the norms of their social environment, whether their mother overdresses, or looks less smart than other mothers, whether they cannot afford to live as their friends do, or whether there is something out of the ordinary in their family life. They are very sensitive about their own appearance and a minor handicap can overshadow their peace of mind and destroy their personal confidence. The embarrassment of being singled out is common experience, but it is particularly painful if the cause is something which draws attention to social inadequacy like "free" school meals or being a member of a minority group. Children are understandably particularly sensitive about their families and about their parents especially. Every child wants to be able to be proud of, or at least pleased with, his parents and how they appear, not only to him but also to other people. He wants them to love him and to be there when he needs them, but he also wants them to be accepted by other children and by other adults as "proper" parents, people he can take for granted as being "OK" and not have to worry about. Some of the painful feelings experienced when this is not possible were described in the previous chapter about family ties. The presence of socially unacceptable parents can cause as much, or nearly as much, pain as the absence of parents altogether, or their infrequent and unpredictable appearances.

For most of the time, most children from ordinarily satisfactory homes, although they are likely to have occasional doubts and anxieties, can rely on a background of parental acceptability as well as reliability within their own social milieu. In many families this background is supported, even in our currently socially and geographically mobile society, by relatives and friends who reinforce feelings of belonging to a group of adults who in the main are kindly disposed towards each other and the children. Family events like Christmas, holidays, parties, anniversaries, weddings and outings add colour and variety to the relatively predictable network of acquaintances, friendships and blood ties within which many children are born and grow up. The disruptions which occur and their concomitant anxieties, sometimes intense, in the most stable of families, are likely to be cushioned, at least to some extent, by members of this network, even when major disasters like divorce or death remove a parent from a child's environment.

If the network of family support is available much that is routine and familiar will continue and the children will not have to face the problems alone, or in totally strange surroundings. Conversely children whose family life breaks down and for whom no supportive wider network remains can be faced not only with the loss of parental care and the confidence that springs from it, but with long term feelings of lack of acceptance by society and damaged identity. Familiar surroundings, people and things are left behind and uncertainties of time, place and future events take their place.

Even the best intentioned social services can seem

impersonal, unpredictable and arbitrary in these circumstances and thoughtless, unimaginative public attitudes can add to the sense of helplessness of children who no longer know the terms of reference of the adults in charge of them. The members of the group remembered clearly the confusing and traumatic nature of their own experiences and how different from other people they had felt as part of the consequences. It was clear from their discussions that they still suffered, not only from the long term effects of childhood loss, but also from the lack of understanding and sensitivity still demonstrated by people who had not shared their experiences.

The years in which they were in public care were between 1942 and 1969. From 1942 to 1948 public assistance, in spite of change and development over three hundred years, retained many traditional poor law attitudes. Its provision was regarded by the Curtis Committee as so lacking in appropriate sensitivity or even basic suitability to the needs of children that their harshest criticisms were directed towards it. When it finally ended in 1948, a long needed opportunity was provided for changes in services, improvement of attitudes in staff and committees, and more appropriate care and support for children in care and their families. These changes, however, had to take place within the community in which other public service and professional groups were expected to provide for children in care as they did for children in their own homes, and in which members of the public were carrying on their own lives, largely unaware of the legislative changes or the needs which had brought them about.

Old attitudes die hard; other people's disasters, particularly when they lead to expenditure of public money, may very easily be seen in judgmental terms and no saying can be more easily demonstrated in real life than that which suggests that the sins of the fathers are visited upon the children. Assisting unmarried mothers could be held to lead to greater numbers of illegitimate children; housing or accommodating homeless families together might encourage failure to pay rent; supporting one-parent families at home without requiring mother or father to work might encourage fecklessness and idle attitudes towards employment. All these approaches to family problems were evident amongst public attitudes in the 1950s and 1960s and affected the lives of children in care and their families. Earlier approaches had been even less sympathetic and public assistance authorities often acted on the belief that children were better off without "bad parents", that is, the homeless, the destitute, the unmarried, and those who had deserted their families or were in prison. To "wipe the slate clean" and start again was thought to be the kindest and most realistic method in the long run. The newly-formed child care service inherited many children in 1948 whose families had been eliminated in this way and many residual, often unconsciously tolerated, features of the old system had to be consciously and persistently whittled away by those who were charged with implementing change. This was difficult enough, but outside the child care service itself change was even more difficult to bring about and was achieved much more slowly. Even where knowledge and motivation to understand existed the rate of change was slow. Where neither the knowledge nor the necessary motivation could be assumed, pressure had to be exerted in many different ways before questioning of traditional practices took place as a preliminary to replacing them.

The implicit attitude of many people to children in care and the whole process of caring for children whose parents were not able to make provision for them was vividly exemplified by the group in their first meeting.

"I think you had some apprehension when mixing with other people. This was sort of inbred in you by the fact that other people regarded you as someone different," said Margaret.

"And they still do, people do now," said Barry.

"They do now," agreed Andrew. "When I mention to

someone, you know I am talking to someone very close, or something like this, it does crop up that I say "Oh, yes — well in my childhood I spent all my life in the Home" and they say "Oh, poor thing" and yet, to me, some of my most enjoyable days, the only days I had in childhood really were in the Home. And I turn round on them in defence, and I think "No, it wasn't, I enjoyed it" and they just can't understand this. They think that you're someone detached from the general community, you're someone different, you know — 'Poor thing, you were in a Home'."

The parents in the group all had a strong sense of not wanting their own children to have to go through the experiences they had had, but it made them angry when people refused to recognise that they themselves had had a mixed experience, not all bad.

"It always raises some anger in me when someone passes a comment like 'Oh, you poor thing, you came from a Home.' I'm immediately ready for argument because I did have a good time," said one member.

"I got up and walked out of an argument like this the other week," responded another member, "because no-one would believe that perhaps we were better off than children in normal homes and I said 'I'm not going to argue with you,' and got up and walked out. I felt terribly childish and silly but I just couldn't get my point over to them and I thought it was pointless to try. I live on a caravan site. We have a lot of children there who are problem children and their mothers are always saying 'Oh, you'll go in a Home if you keep doing things wrong.' And lots of mothers say this to children, 'You'll be put in a children's Home, only naughty children go there and that's where you'll go.' And this is the sort of general attitude with everyone outside."

A group member who was not a parent felt equally strongly:

"Yes, you get these posters as well. I think this is to a large extent how the public are made aware of a children's Home, you have this thing which was appalling to me personally, this poster . . . . I really felt like tearing it down as it gave the impression of a poor, deprived child and we wanted desperately housefathers to come and everyone who hadn't been in a children's Home and didn't know anything about it would really get this impression, that there was really something different about these children. They were a race apart and they were naughty children. I think actually it is largely the way the public has got hold of this. A large amount of play has been put on the spastic which is important because people think, well, a spastic is incapable of living anything but a sub-normal life and therefore you treat him with disrespect, you don't care about the child. You think, well he really is sub-normal, I must stamp on him, and this helps develop the general impression of the children's Home and anything to do with being inside the welfare system as opposed to being outside is bad and depriving and low and a Martian type atmosphere." Alex was associating appeals for handicapped children with his reactions to advertising for residential staff but probably also alluding to the use of spastic as a term of abuse and diminishment in some types of "sick" humour at the time.

Margaret contributed an experience which clearly demonstrated what other members of the group were describing.

"It goes back to where people don't know quite what to think of children in children's Homes or the reasons why they are there and are they different, or aren't they different?" she said.

"It is a big question. I heard a little while ago Cedars House had open evenings and I went over there to see some slides, and I took my children and some other children that lived on the caravan site and this little girl had never seen the inside of a children's Home before. She was ever so frightened when she was going in but there was nothing to be frightened about. I lived there once and I'm out. She thought the doors would be locked when you got there, but when she came out she said 'Can we go again, it was nice there, it was just like an ordinary home, wasn't it?'''

Andrew's experience of being in care had resulted in a
feeling which he described as having "always been at the back
of my mind throughout my life, particularly at school. I often
thought that I was younger than I was, and even at school I
remember thinking when I was perhaps fifteen, or fourteen,
or thirteen, that I was really perhaps about, well, say I was
thirteen I was thinking that perhaps I was ten or eleven or
something like this. Something had gone wrong in my life and
that really I was younger than the class I was in. I felt this."
Martin had had the same feeling so strongly that he had asked
to see his birth certificate. "I found out I am the same age so
I resigned myself to it," he said.

The children's officer asked Andrew how he would have
felt if he had been cared for as though he were a couple of
years younger. "I'd have felt more in my depth I think. I
wouldn't have felt so inadequate at the majority of things."

Martin could verbalize that the feeling of being younger
could be used as an excuse "when you haven't been as good
as anybody else. You think that deep in your mind perhaps
you're a bit younger." Andrew thought the "couldn't-care-
less attitude of the group" fitted in with this too, but they
agreed that seeing a birth certificate could be quite a shock.
"You suddenly come across those years you think you were
behind. It makes you grow up all of a sudden. You start
acting your age then."

For Andrew, seeing his birth certificate at eighteen prior to
going into the services had been a double shock, not only the
official evidence of his age, but also the first intimation that
the name he had always been known by was not the same as
the name on the birth certificate. "It was quite a shock. I was
absolutely shocked, I nearly dropped through the ground."
He had felt sufficiently strongly about the need to retain the
identity he had had to date that he had his name changed by
deed poll to the name by which he had always been known.
Quite understandably he felt this matter should have been
sorted out long before he was eighteen.

The group members had experienced some treatment in schools which made them feel "different". One of them found what she saw as misplaced sensitivity to be a handicap. "I used to long to be like other children that I knew had to take homework home. I would like to have been made to sit down at night and do homework, (but) even at school I found they made allowances for the fact that I was in care and that I came from Canada. Too many allowances; I felt that if only they had come down with a rod of iron it would probably have helped."

"One of the things that does impress on my mind thinking back, is the fact that in a Home we were regarded, to outsiders, school and in the village and things like this, as 'the Home kids'," said Andrew. "At school when there was a medical examination or something like this the teacher used to come out and say 'Now all the Home children stand over this side and all the other ...'" Instead of going forward each with his own class group, the children from his Home were extracted from their individual classes and all put together in a line. "This is where I felt very aware of it. I would rather have been mixed up with the others; I'd have felt more secure that way. You felt that you were detached, you were different, you were something of a Martian, you weren't the same as them and yet you wanted to be the same as them. In anything you were sort of segregated. 'Now the Home people, all the Home people together!' Looking back and trying to remember my feelings at the time, in my own heart I objected to this. I thought 'How can we be different to them? We want to be the same as them.'"

Andrew was describing his experience in the children's Homes and schools he knew. Barry was in a group of children's Homes and a different school but his experience was very similar.

"Everyone knew you were in a children's Home and you tended to be not exactly lined up one side, but that type of thing. I can always remember that one of the things was that you didn't pay for school dinners and other kids looked

strangely at us you know. You weren't one of the other kids
at school really. You came from children's Homes. When I
was fostered out I carried on at the same school and I was still
taken for one of the Homes children; I never went over to the
other side of the grass. When teachers were dealing with
matters in which money and parental permission were
required, school outings, for example, they would say, 'Oh,
you're from the Homes so we needn't bother about you, we'll
find out.' So you'd really got nothing to say in it,"
complained Barry. He found this particularly galling because
he could not remember an instance when the children's
department had not enabled their children to participate in
anything that other children from their own homes were able
to do. "I would have thought that a teacher could probably
have taken our word for it." The children's officer could
explain in the context of this discussion that administrative
arrangements, delegated powers, financial constraints,
committee attitudes were having to be coped with and
modified, but to Barry in his classroom with his peer group
and the teacher, his loss of personal dignity was the
important issue. He resented being made to feel different
from boys in their own homes, and when on one occasion,
without his prior knowledge, arrangements were put in train
for him to go on a six weeks' adventure and education course
in the mountains, which he enjoyed a great deal when he got
there, he was angry that he had not been given a choice. It
was a rare opportunity, only one place for his school and
village, and he realised in retrospect that the social worker
and the school had been involved in positive discrimination,
but no-one likes feeling helpless even when it is for his own
good and fourteen years later Barry remembered the feeling
of helplessness as well as the benefits of the course which was
"marvellous".

Going to church and Sunday school produced similar
problems. Because there were a number of children going at a
particular time, it seemed they inevitably set out as a group
from the Home and walked through the village together.

"We were always aware that we were a separate group by this fact. I felt that way because we were all going in a group like a swarm of bees. You felt that people were looking at you, staring at you as you went past."

It was not only in children's Homes that the group's experience made them feel "different". Carol had been adopted but "my Mum has got her own daughter and I have always felt inferior to her because, if anybody used to come to the house she used to introduce her and then she'd sort of say 'Oh, well there's my adopted daughter' or something to that effect and I used to feel that I was different. I've never really been able to talk to my mother, it was very difficult to get through to anybody." Although only four when placed in her foster home from a residential nursery, Carol had vague memories of her introductory visits to it. She remembered she had left a toy, "a dog or a donkey or something" at the foster home on one of these visits. She also remembered being adopted at five years old.

"I remember the Town Hall. I'd been a little bit of a bitch I think, I'd been naughty anyway and I kept rattling things about, that's all I can remember." The foster home, though an adoptive home to her, had continued to take short-term foster children.

"I think I was always a bit bewildered because of so many children coming and going. I can remember mother had a little girl while her mother was in hospital having another one, and Mum telling me that she would be going back to her mother and I thought this was going to happen to me. I was a bit upset about it. With children coming and going I thought I was going to go."

Looking back Carol felt that children who were fostered or adopted stood out in a small village "and the children at the primary school used to jeer at you, 'they're not her real parents, she hasn't got a Mum and Dad like us,' all this sort of thing. It leaves an imprint on your mind! I think I would have been better off left in a children's Home to be with other children who were in the same position with me."

Even when Carol went to a technical college the problem was still there. "I don't know how some of the kids in my class found out that I'd been adopted but they used to feel sorry for me. I didn't want anybody to feel sorry for me."

Sometimes being in care not only felt "different" but was seen as punishment. Valerie going home for weekends from the observation and assessment centre, was threatened she would be sent back if she didn't behave herself. "It really made me feel as though I was being punished." Not until after she went out of care, was she able to understand, and more important, believe, that the people caring for her, many of whom she said she liked, were concerned about her for her own sake and not because she was being punished.

A number of the group, looking back, felt their whole life had changed in quality and development as a result of their having to be cared for away from their homes.

"I left my childhood behind when I went into care because I haven't got a thing that I had when I was very young." This was how Anne described what to her had seemed an abrupt loss of identity, the beginning of feeling different from how she would have felt if her own home had remained. She explained that it was not so much being moved about from place to place that worried her, but the changes of people, "the feeling that a bit of me was being left behind in each place or with each lot of people. Every time somebody went out of my life, a bit of me was there, left behind too. Probably why I look back so much was because I wanted those bits, I wanted to feel a whole person again. Even now I suppose I don't really feel a whole person, I feel as though there's something people have got that I haven't, something indefinable, something I cannot place. I feel as though I haven't got it and am lost without it. Maybe its something to do with lack of security, you know." After her mother left them, Anne had gradually accepted and learned to depend on the residential staff who cared for her. Believing, however, that her brother would benefit from fostering she steeled herself to give them up too and thereby reinforced her feelings of loss, not only of other people, but of her own childhood self.

"I suppose leaving the children's Home to stay with my foster parents was more of an adult step to me, as though I was actually turning my back on childhood because I never at any time after that felt young. I felt quite mature and great things were expected of me which I consequently tried to do, you know, most times failing, but I didn't feel young after that. No more mucking about. I mean you see kids of sixteen and seventeen today and they don't give a damn for other people's attitudes when it comes to enjoying themselves. They stand in groups and talk and natter on, and laugh and joke. At that age, I couldn't stand the crowd, I couldn't even listen, you know, very timid I was! I felt remote from any body my own age group, as though I had passed that stage, felt more advanced than they were, although I can't remember living through this age, unless that was when I was twelve or thirteen, when I first went into secondary modern school. I remember feeling very small, in fact we were always feeling very small."

Anne was in fact a large child for her age and the conflict of her inner feelings of smallness, her external size which led to expectations which were often greater than she could meet, and the demands she made on herself were vividly expressed to the group: "I feel as though I've always been grown up, and, on the other hand, I feel as though I'm never going to grow up."

Another member of the group described his general state of mind while in care as feeling out his depth. Margaret called it a "mesmerized state". Describing how she related to the residential staff in her children's Home she said, "I could talk to almost anybody but I'd never say anything really secret to any of them. I don't think I had any real deep thoughts about anything, I mean I was in a mesmerized state I suppose really." Asked whether she meant she was deliberately trying to keep things going on the surface, she replied "I don't think I knew I was doing it. I remember feeling rather bewildered for quite a long time and I wanted to do so much and I couldn't do things and yet I can't tell you what I wanted to do. There was nothing very deep in my thoughts, it was everyday thoughts and never got to the bottom of thinking why did I do so-and-so, or why should I do so-and-so or why shouldn't I, which most children do. They think about this." She based this latter statement on "having worked with children and my own little lad. He turns round and says 'why should I?' I didn't ask many questions and accepted what went on."

Derek seemed to be demonstrating the same problem when he described his inability to confide in anyone. As a tiny child in the children's Home (he left when he was six) he recalled "I used to spend half my time in the toilet actually, standing on the seat looking out of the window at the cars going by to the local. I used to go up there when I had a problem or something. I'd go up looking all gloomy and come down smiling. I used to like being on my own. I still do when I have a problem to sort out. Some people don't need people to talk to. I used to talk to a big elephant once when I had a problem, — I used to tell my troubles to that. I used to punch it when I had a few problems, and that was one of my personal toys."

"Were you able to take it with you?"

"Not to the lavatory."

"I mean when you left the home."

"No, that was one of the things I missed, actually."

"What made you single out the elephant?"

"I don't know, I used to like it first of all, I suppose. I used to ride it. I can imagine it lying in a corner after I left, all the stuffing knocked out of it. I knew it was a toy but it used to take a bit of punching when I was trying to get back at somebody who was bigger than I was."

Even when he was fostered and even though he knew it hurt his foster mother, he could not confide in anyone. "I used to try to keep my face up, you know, not to be soft by telling all my troubles out like that."

Barry agreed that he had had the same difficulty and that he had stopped being able to confide in anyone when he was told that "I wasn't going back home again."

Miranda's social worker tried many ways of helping her to resolve some of her feelings of resentment about what she had missed in life as a child. Talking about the past was one way. To facilitate this she had taken her back to the building in which she had lived from a couple of weeks old to about two years. At that time it was a residential nursery; when Miranda revisited it, it was a children's Home and she had never been there since she left. As soon as she entered she had said "I remember there was a rocking horse somewhere." Enquiry confirmed that it was in the attic though neither staff nor children had seen it for years. "We used to pull the tail out and stuff marbles in it so that when you rocked it, it made a lot of noise," said twenty-year-old Miranda. Her memories were vivid, imprinted by the emotions of a child, and still so painful that she changed her christian name when she went out of care "because I just wanted to start afresh." "I seem to get on much better with everybody all round now that I'm out of care," she told the group, "mainly because I knew I was in care and I had all these people to answer to, but now that I am my own responsibility and I can choose who I want as friends and choose what I want to do without having to ask anyone I seem to get on a lot better."

Miranda had hated her lot and saw life beginning for her when she was no longer a child.

On the other hand some members of the group clung to mementoes of their childhood, like Derek who told them "I was just remembering about three years after I went into adoption (that is, left the children's Home), after I had learned to wander about by myself, I used to go down to Riverside just to look around to see if there was anybody I remembered, and I took a big chunk out of the wall, and I've still got it. In fact I heard the place is going to be pulled down in the future. I think I'll get in first and ask for the name plate. The chunk of wall is out in the shed somewhere, I

wouldn't throw it out." A piece of brick or stone can help to
retain a sense of identity and continuity in a fragmented life.
Most children can reinforce their own identity and sense of
continuity by talking about home. Derek could not and nor
could Barry, although he remembered more about his home.
He could not talk about it for different reasons. He explained
that when he moved from the reception Home to the group of
Homes "every grown-up face around you was a different
one, and I think you probably think that there are so many
kids there and you are just another number and if you asked
someone they wouldn't know much about you anyway. You
might feel this at the time and I can't remember anyone
asking me where I came from or anything."

"Did it not occur to you that they may have been told?"

"Not at the time, no. If someone doesn't ask you
something, well, at the time I thought, they don't sort of
know much about you."

A family nearby, where he used to visit a friend of his own
age, was a place where he could talk because they talked to
him about his family.

Andrew had no conscious family memories of his father
and mother, though he was very conscious of his need for
them. It made him value the interest shown in him by a
member of the domestic staff of his children's Home. "I had
the feeling that she was more motherly to me than ever a
mother could be in my mind. She gave me a photograph of
herself at some stage whilst I was in the Home and I
remember I looked at it several times after I left. I've really
got some sort of attachment for her. I don't remember her
name but I once visited the place where she lived and
apparently she's moved now. The people at the house didn't
know where she had gone. I know I had a job years after . . . .
I'd lost the photograph and everything." When Andrew had
first gone into lodgings and was very lonely, "I remember I
often used to, at odd moments, get the photograph out and
look at it and obviously I must have had a great attachment
to her in a funny sort of way, because it wasn't even as if she

was there twenty-four hours a day, she must have worked an eight or nine hours day there, and yet I could have so much for her."

Looking back Andrew expressed the view that "It seems to be vitally important that everything is done to avoid any thought of being any different than any other child."

Martin's experience tended to confirm the research which suggests the earlier the placement the more secure it is likely to be, but although he regarded his foster home as his home, a certain determination to have as little as possible to do with potential disrupters was evident in his technique of dealing with child care officers and was perhaps some indication of wanting to feel the same as other children. He had been placed as a small baby with a childless couple.

"It worked out very well, there was nothing I could do about it and that was it. I was there and I was happy and they seemed happy, so that was fair enough. It gave me another life and it gave them life where there was no chance of life; it worked out well for me. I'm one of the lucky ones. I didn't get any thought of being moved because I was so small, and I grew up and time was going on, and nobody had ever said anything about being moved, so I naturally thought nothing would happen."

"Did you have any doubts or worries about the visits of child care officers to your house?" "No, if they could catch me in they were lucky."

Martin's foster parents had consulted him about whether he would like to change his name to theirs, but in his down-to-earth way he "decided to keep it to what it was and that was it, sort of thing. I haven't pressed the matter."

So at school he was known by his own name, but unlike some of the others, perhaps partly because he was so integrated into his foster home and its wider circle of relatives and friends, although he experienced children asking questions, he would shrug them off and say nothing.

The state of being mesmerized described above may have been contributed to by the way in which things happened when members of the group were in care. Often "things seemed to be illogical, there was just no reason for so many things that happened." The speaker wished it had been possible to know "what were the important things as opposed to the unimportant things. This goes back to the fact that I didn't really get an understanding with anyone because I thought that everyone was leaving me to go my own way. I never realized that I was so obstinate, or seemed so obstinate," said Margaret.

Discussion of the problem of children in care not knowing how the social services work brought the comment that "the only security you have got when you are in care is that that is given to you from the people above. Where you happen to live and the bed you happen to sleep in isn't your bed, because if you move from there somebody else will have it. Nothing is ever completely yours, other than perhaps a few possessions that you have got."

The group made many comments about the way in which the staff of the child care service worked and how they appeared to them. Amongst their experiences of being "different" was the lack of what they saw as adequate personal contact and involvement with adults. They commented on the detachment of social workers' attitudes as perceived by them. One of them preferred the children's officer's way, not of asking them what they wanted to do, but telling them what she wanted them to do. It was taken as a sign of involvement and caring. Even loss of temper might demonstrate care: "Well, when a person loses her temper with them (that is, children) they realise how they are really involved in their case" — though "for a younger child I think it wants somebody who doesn't lose their temper."

"I got the impression with my own children at certain stages of their life, particularly with the youngest now, that they want a smacking; they get into a tantrum and they want you to smack them, and pull them up short," said Andrew.

Children in care, one of the group commented, also realize that the adults looking after them have to answer to someone else; "the big white goddess" was the term they half jokingly used, whereas children in their own homes know "their parents haven't got to answer to anybody higher up." Another member followed this point by explaining from his own experience that "if foster parents accept you as their own child, do you not want to live in the same atmosphere as their own child, like a married couple would have their own children? They would squabble and fight, you as a foster child would also want to live in that family atmosphere and also squabble and fight, and not be segregated because they have got to be good, because they have got somebody here (in the children's department) to keep an eye on them. They have got their own life and they want to lead it the same as another family."

The experiences the members of the group shared with each other demonstrated that they felt "different" not only because they had lost so much of what most children can take for granted but also that their sense of being different was often unintentionally reinforced by methods of care, by attitudes of other services and by public attitudes conveyed through other children and the communities in which they lived. To the pain of bereavement, shock, disappointment, disillusion and rejection was added the unexplained stigma of being "different" bringing with it feelings of inadequacy, lack of confidence, even a sense of guilty responsibility for events and people involved in their life situation.

In this and the previous chapter group members' experiences and feelings about families and separation from them have been explored. The following chapters are focussed on the services that provided them with care; the residential establishments they lived in, the social workers who were in contact with their families and others, the foster and adoptive homes and lodgings which took them in, and the teachers and schools concerned with their education. They had been asked by the children's officer to share their experience with her and her two colleagues because of the light they might throw on the consumers' perceptions of what was provided. In doing so they had to name people and establishments and were anxious that this should not cause embarrassment or pain to anyone they had known. They were assured that care would be taken to avoid identification, and with that assurance felt free to contribute their memories, comments and proposals for improved services based on the experience of what they themselves received. In the main they expressed considerable understanding of the difficulties of professional staff in carrying out their caring tasks, and were tolerant of failures to meet their own needs though they regretted them and often recognised them clearly. Their own unhappiness had not made them bitter about people who provided services though some had bitter feelings about the shadows on their own lives. In fact, perhaps because life had dealt with them hardly, they appeared to accept its unevenness and unfairness with less rancour than anyone would have been entitled to expect from them. This did not, however, make them uncritical in their assessments nor unquestioning of the organisation and system of services. Some of their questions were for the purpose of clarifying issues which had puzzled them in the past, but some were related to understanding and commenting on current services.

5 Residential Care — Children's Homes

All the members of the group at some time were in residential care, though one who was placed in a foster home as a baby had no recollection of it. Most of the others had clear memories and could draw on them extensively. In addition all of them had had experience of field social workers whose role in relation to them ran right through everything that happened, from the time before they left home and through whatever form of substitute care they subsequently received until they reached eighteen years of age. It might, therefore, have been logical to see first what the group's experience of field social workers had been before looking at other forms of service. On the other hand the first conscious experience of full-time care which the majority of the group had had was in a residential Home and was the one therefore in which they experienced the first full impact of being away from their own homes. For some it was also the means by which their needs were provided for on a long-term as well as on a short-term basis. In addition, like foster homes and adoption, residential care is all embracing in the sense that being at home is an all-embracing situation, living, sleeping, eating, playing, sharing a joint life with other people. By comparison field social workers, though their impact on group members' lives was very significant, spent very little time with them individually and had no direct responsibility for meeting their everyday human needs. For these reasons the group members' experience of the substitute care provided by residential establishments, including children's Homes, hostels, boarding educational establishments and a partially secure psychiatric hospital is examined first. The hospital was unique in the life of one member of the group, but it was a residential experience and one which related closely to the reason for that member being in care. By its similarity and contrasts it threw into relief some of the other experiences of residential care which she and other members had had.

Residential work for children changed radically during the first few years after 1948. The Curtis Committee had been so concerned about the lack of training in child care that an interim report was published before the final recommendations which led to the Children Act of 1948.[1] They also emphasized the importance to children of small family groups, preferably in the charge of a married couple, where children could be more closely in touch with the experiences of everyday life. In an environment on this scale, the woman would "play the part of a mother to the children", while the man "must play the father . . . (pursuing) out-of-door and recreational activities rather than physical care of the child."[2]

"Children's departments inherited a huge legacy of large institutions, that would be hard to sell, and expensive to replace. Nevertheless, reduction in the size of children's homes and the gradual closure or adaptation of old institutions was attempted by many authorities, and encouraged by the Home Office."[3] In the local authority in which members of the group were in care several old institutions were closed in the early years of the child care service and new properties purchased. "The inherited cottage homes which were thought unsuitable and isolated were finally disposed of in 1956" but "the very small children's home was never adopted. . . . Instead of very small units, children's homes for twenty or thirty were adapted to house small 'family groups' where children had their own special rooms and their own special members of staff attached. The authority was hesitant to commit itself to the Curtis model, seeing the difficulties in placing some large families together in the smaller homes, and anticipating greater staffing difficulties. The small size of family group homes made it difficult to pay high enough salaries to attract qualified staff (the level of remuneration was tied to the number of beds) and where the burden of care rested on only two or three people, turnover could result in considerable disruption for the children.''[4]

It would be impossible to say how many staff in all were involved in the residential establishments in which members of the group lived at various times, but some of them were remembered vividly and were of considerable significance to the members in their experience as children in care. Forty-two residential staff and a doctor in the psychiatric hospital were remembered by name. Many more, like some of the staff of two residential nurseries, three boarding educational establishments and the domestic staff of these and other homes were mentioned but not named. Because forty-two people were named it is possible to provide some information about them. The majority, thirty-one, had received no special training for their work, though one of them was a qualified field social worker, one a qualified nurse and two were qualified teachers. The eleven others had received training for residential work, nine on general courses, one on a course for work with adolescents and one on a senior course designed for very experienced staff. Seven of these eleven were employed as heads of homes or deputies. The members of the group who had known these residential staff were unaware of which had received training and which had not, nor in the main did they know anything about them beyond their day-to-day experience together. Their memories and comments related to this and how far the residential group life had met their own needs. Knowing that the identity of members of staff would be protected they felt free to share experience and feelings about a number of individuals as well as more general memories and impressions.

Andrew had had the earliest experience of any of the group

since his years in care spanned the last years of public assistance services and the first years of child care. He felt it very important that there was "someone with a fatherly instinct or someone you could look to as a father, but (who) enjoyed the same sort of outlets that you wanted to develop, sport and things like that." He also felt strongly that there should be "more resident people" to "take an interest individually" in the children. "There certainly wasn't enough in my time." Andrew had some very institutional memories. Describing his first children's Home he said, "One of the worst things I remember was the fact that if you misbehaved — we had a big hut that we used to congregate and play in, and if you misbehaved yourself, winter or summer or whatever weather it was, you were made to stand out on the step. It seemed to me like hours on end, with your hands behind your head like this. This was in the winter too. I remember the frost being on the lawn and staring out there. We were rapped if we took our hands from behind our heads. It seemed like hours to me, possibly it was only half an hour but this is something I remember and I thought it was wrong."

On another occasion "I remember when we were distributed with Red Cross parcels, and I remember there was an American, with an American attitude with his ciné camera and all the rest of it, and all us children were out on the lawn. I remember being absolutely enthralled by the fact that I had been taken on the ciné camera and they came back some time later and ran off the film and there was I opening my Red Cross box frantically and the first thing on the top was a net, something like net headscarves, in the shape of a Union Jack, you know, it had the Union Jack's colours on it. And there I was holding up the Union Jack, very proud. This is one of the earliest memories I have and it's very vivid to me. I didn't have very happy memories of Pine Lodge." Whilst there he had experienced "some of the things that you'd do to prisoners rather than children." He thought the staff "were more concerned with themselves than they were with us children. There was a matronly atmosphere as opposed to a substitute father/mother atmosphere." When the Home was closed he moved to another: "as soon as I got to The Beeches I felt very happy straight away; like a fish in water again."

Andrew had "some very happy times" with the superintendent there. "I suppose he could have had an ordinary saloon (car) but he chose a big Land Rover, I think mainly for the purpose that he could take us children out on outings and things like this and us boys used to enjoy it immensely going out with him."

Barry also had happy memories of a couple in one of the children's Homes he was in. The husband was "a man that enjoyed sport. Most boys like sport and anything in the sporting line we did. I think it makes a lot of difference, the sport side of it. It did to us." "You can be in a Home where everyone is happy," he asserted. Asked to enlarge on this he went on, "The Home where the Adams were in charge it seemed to me that all the staff were interested in you, even the cleaners, and you were allowed to talk to them, and they were allowed to talk to you and everyone seemed to get on. We actually called the Adams Mummy and Daddy and really they seemed as though they were. They treated us all as their own sons. We thought they were wonderful. I think our world fell apart when they left."

He was later cared for by another couple about whom he had very mixed feelings. "I don't think I really liked them." They had a baby whom the boys enjoyed pushing out round the village in his pram but some of the things they did were so "way out" the children did not know how to take them. They insisted on being called by their christian names, but in addition, because the Home was not adequately supplied with play equipment they did "such mad things" which although the children enjoyed them made them very anxious. "You didn't know quite how to take them. If you wanted to do something you were just allowed to do it. I can't remember the actual things we did but one things really stands out. I can remember we had a gorgeous tent on the lawn with umpteen blankets and everything in it. This all came off the beds in our own dormitory! They also had a lot of old clothes and things and we used to dress up a lot and ran about all over the place.'' This couple were in charge of the Home but "there were still some of the other, I can't remember, did we call the other people aunts?'' Barry asked. "Some of them stayed and this helped us get over the Miriam and Sam part I think. It was so strange. It came suddenly. Everything seemed to change.''

The problem of change manifested itself in various ways. For children the difficulty of establishing confidence may be increased by the mystery of events happening not only to them but also to others. One member of the group described some of the comings and goings of himself, his brothers and other boys during the time he was in children's Homes.

"I had three brothers with me at the Cedars and I think we were still just the same as being at home, you know, a family. Then one brother must have been about school leaving age because he went into Barsetshire I think; I didn't know where at the time. Then the three of us went to Riverside and the youngest brother went into Essex House, and the other two of us went into Winston. We weren't very happy at him being taken away from us then, I can remember. At first we didn't know why, but then we seemed to think it was because he was so much younger than us. Then Edwin left and went off to work. While we were there, a group of the boys, and Edwin was one of them, were sent to the remand home. No one knew why they went. I can't remember how long they were away, a couple of weeks or something. Then Edwin came back and then he left and went to work. I think he went to Oddingley and then Toby (his third brother) stayed in Essex House and I stayed in Winston.''

Andrew described the disappearance of a member of staff to whom he had become very attached at The Beeches, "One minute he was there and the next gone. I had the feeling that he got married although I don't know whether he did or not.'' Margaret responded, "Talking about people being there one minute and not the next, I seem to have been through this with everyone in care, including children. People did seem to disappear all of a sudden for no particular reason, and you talking about it, I never realised that I thought about it before, but I must have done. Thinking back to the different people I met, there seemed to be so many people just milling about and they'd all drift off one by one, no-one seemed to know why or where."

One of the professional members of the group asked, "Why do you think you accepted it then?"

"Because so many people were doing it," said Margaret. "If one individual had disappeared out of our lives then we would probably have noticed it a lot more but both staff and children did the same. And places, you went to one place and then you went to another place, and you always seemed to be on the move. Everyone seemed to be on the move."

"I don't think it is a good thing all these sudden changes," Andrew went on, "because I didn't really get attached to anyone as completely as I could have done, mainly because of the fact that things changed too often. Even if you take staff, you get used to faces, people, they almost seem to feel one of you in some respects, and then there's a new face there and the old one's departed. At the time it doesn't seem to register very much with you but on reflection obviously it must have some effect, perhaps leads to a little bit of withdrawal, although you don't feel it in yourself at the time. It creates a hard shell on you and each time this happens the shell gets a little harder. In going into marriage I have always had it in the back of my mind, that I should forever beware that my children should never have the same circumstances that I had."

"I think I went through almost the same as that and I was petrified of having any children," said Margaret.

Responding to this feeling another member said, "It must take a child a long time to get used to a different way of life and it would be much easier if they could visit where they were going to go and be reassured that they were not just being sent away because nobody wanted them.''

Yet even when this happens it does not deal with all the anxiety as another member demonstrated when he recalled how he was taken to see a residential establishment in another part of the country so that he could understand and discuss the decision which had been made about his future. The visit involved two long journeys with his child care officer who was experienced and well trained. Alex was an intelligent boy whose father, he knew, had been involved in the decision and had agreed to it in view of Alex's problems at day school as well as all the other factors involved in his life. Nevertheless he said, ''I think the only thing I ever wondered about was why I was actually moving. Now I know, I can understand that now, but at the time I couldn't quite grasp the idea behind it. It was rather frightening actually because my father used to come and visit me every weekend practically at The Cedars and I realised that in Downshire this would not be possible.''

What staff in Homes were called was an issue raised in the first meeting of the group. Alex had suggested then that it did not matter what people were called, it was ''the amount of love or respect'' that mattered. One of the professional staff described a boy she knew, not one of the group, who lived in a children's Home where the staff suggested the children call them ''Mum and Dad'' if they wished to. This boy had chosen to do so, because he said ''If I don't call you Mum and Dad there will be nobody ever in my life I'll be able to call Mum and Dad.''

Two housemothers had remained in the hearts of some of the group. Auntie Mabel was one. ''We took to her,'' said Barry. ''I think she was a mainstay at that time actually'' (that is, when the ''way out'' couple were in charge). ''She used to have us doing all sorts of things. I can remember we used to sit for hours doing embroidery. We were all boys but we enjoyed doing it. It was her attitude. She never told you to do anything; she asked you to do it and, I don't know, she was just a motherly sort. Anything she wanted you to do you just got up and did it and that was that. We liked being with her.''

Another housemother had also been much loved by the children. ''She looked very severe and very strict. After I had been there a few weeks I found she was the best one. She seemed to have a soft spot for the children, you could turn to her. If you were crying you could turn to her and tell her why and she would listen to your explanation and say, ''Well come on then, let's go and see,'' not ''I don't believe you.'' She just had a different approach, she made you feel that you weren't as stupid as the Thackers liked you to feel. They sort of (said) ''Oh well, we are looking after you, you will do as we say. If we say you are lying you are lying.''

''Yes, they had set their path and nothing wavered with them,'' said Margaret.

''We're not saying that with Auntie Clare you got your own way all the time,'' Barry responded.

''Oh no, if you were wrong you were told off,'' replied Margaret. ''She had the same sort of discipline as the Thackers but in a different sort of way, an acceptable sort of way. Whether I was right or wrong I just felt that I wanted to explain what had really happened. I used to scheme as to what I would do that would annoy them as much as they annoyed me. I used to think ''I won't go home'' or else I used to sneak out. I wouldn't have even considered doing it if Auntie Clare was on duty. I would go down and say ''Can we go there?'' and she would have said ''Yes, as long as you are not too long.''

''I couldn't stand them,'' continued Margaret. ''Do you remember,'' she said turning to the children's officer, ''me phoning you up and saying ''I've got to get away from this house?'' ''

''We used to call him ''bulldog'','' Barry commented, ''He was a bit like one. He barked terribly.''

''In fact after a time you didn't try to tell them anything, you just went under them to Auntie Clare,'' concluded Margaret.

This couple were unpopular because of their authoritarian manner and the over-emphasis they put on what the children saw as unimportant. The children also hated being accused of lying when they were not.

"They tended to throw their weight about rather a lot especially over shoe cleaning. We took it in turns to clean everybody's shoes and if one pair had any marks on it, you would get the slipper even. They were fond of giving you the slipper, oh yes, they were very fond of it."

"And telling you that you were telling lies. If your shoes were damp and you cannot clean shoes that are damp, they won't shine, you were lying. Even if you had been through the whole lot and cleaned them twice, you were still lying if you hadn't got a good shine on every pair of shoes. You were made to stay there until you did it and if you answered back then it was bed. I got sent to bed without any tea on one occasion when I would have thought if they had looked they could have seen I wasn't lying."

"Did you used to feel sorry for yourself afterwards?" asked another group member.

"No, I just used to think, 'Oh, the stupid fool!' replied Margaret.

"They always seemed so high and mighty, you couldn't get through to them. On the other hand they were sociable themselves, there were always people about in there. If you saw a strange person floating about it was someone to see Mr and Mrs Thacker, and letting you have anyone you liked into tea provided you said 'Can they come to tea tomorrow?' was one of the things the Thackers were good at. If you had a friend and it was your turn to butter the bread or something, if your friends came to tea then they'd go in the kitchen and help you butter the bread."

Carol had been under five years old when she left the residential nursery in which she spent the first years of her life. Her memories were less than a number of the others but she recalled a few incidents. One of them was when, as she described it, the children had been pushed out to play after they had had breakfast although it had been snowing. "We had been put out to play in the snow and we were so cold we wanted to come in but they had closed the doors and wouldn't let us come in. This has always stuck in the back of my mind."

Miranda had a similar memory though she had been older than Carol at the time. It was when Mrs Moseley had got so tired of "us banging on the windows and doors one day, she got us all in a line and took us all the way down towards Wateley and right round Longford and back down Weston and that is a walk! We were frozen to the bone!"

Mrs Moseley was the wife of the couple in charge of Miranda's children's Home and the memory sparked off in Miranda by Carol's story was very unusual in her experience of "Auntie" as she called Mrs Moseley. "I got on so well with Auntie," Miranda said. "She would tell me if I was being a b_____ as she put it. I didn't like her for saying it but it's afterwards you appreciate it. I think she must have liked me, that's what I felt; I just felt I could communicate with Auntie." Miranda was very attached to Auntie, but felt differently about the housemother in charge of her group. She was someone "with Charles Dickens ideas about behaviour." Miranda recalled an example which involved a little boy in the same group as herself.

"She used to give us malt and cod liver oil, that horrible sticky stuff in a big jar. I didn't mind it but the rest of them hated it and this little boy did. I remember once she forced it down his throat, holding his nose and pulling his hair back. I was so shocked at what she was doing I just stood up and said 'what do you think you are doing?' He was being sick and everything because he didn't want the stuff. I looked at the others and they were feeling the way I was feeling and we all just stood up and walked out. We didn't speak to her for about two hours we were so shocked."

"What happened to the little boy?" asked the children's officer.

"Oh, poor little thing, he was just sick."

Miranda had been this housemother's "right hand girl" for a time but because "I liked to think I was helping because I wanted to help, not because she wanted me to help, I was demoted. Through that, I think I began to dislike her and began to see what she was about. She had this thing in a drawer, I think you call it a cat with nine tails and if we were naughty, like I didn't like custard, I just didn't like it, I was just sick, and just couldn't stand it, she used to make me eat it and she used to hold this thing above me to make sure I did. You know, thirteen leather straps on it. She never used it, but she did this to frighten us into doing it."

The problem of whether children could, or should, complain about things they felt were wrong or unjust was discussed by the group. What would be the outcome if they did complain? Miranda had once been outside the children's Home putting her bike together and had heard three members of staff talking together about Auntie. "I didn't like what they were talking about so I went in and told them. I didn't half get a wallop; I threatened I would tell Auntie. I said 'I don't care what you say out of earshot but you want to be careful!' I remember we were going to the pantomime and Brenda, my housemother, was going on at me so I said 'I'll tell Auntie what you said in the laundry room' and she held my arm really hard so I kicked her and ran ahead and caught Auntie up. I told her in the end and she didn't believe me. I now think it must have been quite hurtful that I told her that, but at the time I didn't realise. This is why I could never communicate because what you said to one was said to everybody else, you couldn't really let yourself go, but I was fortunate because I could tell Auntie. If she was off duty you weren't allowed to go to speak to her, no matter how desperate it was, even if she was in her room, but I used to. I used to creep up and say 'Auntie, let me in, I want to tell you something'."

Miranda's memories of children's agonies about food they detested reminded Margaret of a little boy in her children's Home who disliked fish but nevertheless was forced to eat it.

"He must have dreaded Friday. He used to cry, he used to throw up at the table and everything but he had to sit and eat it. He wasn't given just a tiny bit, he was given as much as the rest of us." She did not remember that this little boy was able to complain to anyone outside the Home. But when Mrs Thacker spoke, as she thought, unkindly, about Margaret's mother, although Margaret did not admire her mother, she complained.

"I was making the beds with Mrs Thacker one day and I can't remember how it came up (but) she turned round and said, 'Oh, you'll never go back to your mother. Your mother's completely mad.' Well of course I saw red at this and ended up by getting thumped by her and I hurt my elbow by going through a wardrobe door. That was it, I wasn't going to take that. I wasn't very forthright at sticking up for myself, but I went down to Auntie Clare and I said 'What am I going to do, I can't take her, I don't want to know her.' And she said 'Go and phone up your child care officer.' She wasn't going to take sides so I thought 'Right, where do I get the money? How do I use the telephone anyway?' Whether I wrote or whether I came over (to the children's department office) I can't remember but Miss Brown came straight over (to the children's Home) within a very short time and talked to me and I felt as though they had done something about it."

Valerie, on the other hand, as an adolescent in a psychiatric hospital, even with a very supportive social worker, had not felt it worth while to complain of the hospital clothes she had to wear "1910 I should think," nor of only being able to have a clean pair of knickers once a week, and one bath a week. She had complained to the Sister on the ward, who had said there was no money for luxuries. Valerie claimed her own clothes were in her case locked up in a store room because patients were not allowed to wear their own clothes.

Another member of the group after she became an adult experienced official unwillingness to listen to complaints. She had been working in a children's Home where the treatment of the children was as impersonal and high-handed as she felt the treatment she had received herself from the Thackers had been. She had taken the trouble to speak to the children's department about it but "I think she (the children's officer) thought I was being childish." One of the professional staff in the group from her own experience, demonstrated how powerless a child may feel. The little boy she was describing was seven and thought he had been unjustly accused of something in the children's Home where he was living. They had had a long conversation in which she had discussed with him what might be done, but at the end of it he said, "but of course you know there is nothing you can do because what is one little boy against all those aunties?"

Miranda had been more fearless and outspoken than most as a child but as she pointed out to the children's officer, she had not succeeded in persuading her to listen sympathetically enough to her complaints about her boarding school to take action and remove her. Only when external events had indicated clearly that the school was no longer suitable had her social worker and the children's officer brought her back to her long-term home at The Beeches. This was an illustration of how easy it is to ignore the messages that children are trying to give.

In general discussion of the problem of complaints (which was not limited to residential settings) the group was aware of the complexities of the issue; the problem of complaints made from malice and the hurt they can cause, the genuine complaints ignored for apparently good reasons, the reluctance of neighbours to be involved, the possibility of public authorities ignoring the point of view of the recipients of services and the risks inherent in some situations. They also knew from their own experience the problem of assessing a residential establishment from outside. One of them put it like this:

"I personally don't think you can really tell what even a residential establishment that you visit often is completely like unless you live in. This is just the difficulty that you've

always got in running establishments of this kind.''
Miranda's story about her housemother's "cat with nine
tails" had not previously been known outside her children's
Home, nor had the practices of making children eat foods
they detested. On the other hand, group members were able
to see that children might attempt to play off their field social
workers against the residential staff caring for them, and that
it might be desirable and necessary for child, residential and
field work staff to discuss things together. Looking back on
the incident when Mrs Thacker spoke unkindly of her
mother, Margaret said, "I don't suppose it was really her
fault looking back on it now, but at the time I felt she was
being really nasty and really horrible, but having spoken
about it here I'm beginning to wonder who was the nastiest of
all, whether it was me because of what I had read into what
she'd said, and I've always held this against them. Perhaps I
shouldn't, perhaps it was me.''

Another member thought that one of the possible solutions
was that the contact between field social workers and the
children for whom they had a responsibility "should be more
close." "You try to put yourself in their shoes and say, 'Well
how would I feel?' . It's very difficult to be able to do this; in
some cases it's virtually impossible, but I think that all the
time you've got to try and do it.''

It was common ground that every child in care needed at
least one adult to act as an encouraging and special person to
that child. It could be someone in a residential establishment
or someone outside, but, said Andrew, "I think it's got to be
somebody you've got a feeling for, somebody you could
confide in, whom you feel you could gain encouragement
from, and you want to please.''

"Yes," said Martin, "you could start off with that feeling
of wanting to please first of all and then you'd realise later on
that it was doing you good as well.''

"Yes, it suddenly dawns on you, doesn't it?" replied
Andrew.

"When you're old enough to realise it," Martin agreed.

One of the most poignant contributions made by a member of the group underlined the need children have for someone in whom they can safely confide, someone who is prepared to give them special attention and comfort in distress. It also illustrated how children often need residential social workers to play a substitute parenting role whether those staff wish to or not, whether it is considered professional or not. Anne and her brother and sister had been deserted by their mother and were initially placed together in a small children's Home where Anne thought they were only going to stay for a short time. Anne remembered two housemasters in particular there, one because "she looked vaguely like Mum, I thought, with dark hair and she was slim." The other she remembered because of the comfort she gave when Anne was in despair. Anne had gradually got the idea that she was going to be in the Home for a long time and "got very upset at nights. I used to cry for hours. I used to be heartbroken sometimes. It was my mother really, being aware that she wasn't going to come back and I couldn't take it. I wouldn't live with it, I suppose. I don't think I wanted to live with it. I just wanted to cry and cry and never wake up in the morning. It was the only outlet for me, I didn't try to be aggressive or anything, though sometimes I was. I remember sometimes making myself cry because I thought 'If you don't cry, you are going to do something else!' And I deliberately imagined my mother walking away down the road. I suppose I made myself cry imagining that, and then if nobody came in I would cry louder and louder until somebody did come in. I suppose really it was my mother's arms I wanted, you know, more than anything. It was nearly always Auntie Betty (who came in). She was a bit of a bible sometimes (the housemother was very religious) but I adored her for when she used to come in at nights."

A little later a married couple whom they called Mum and Dad Todd came to look after Ann and the others. They were much loved. "She was Mum as soon as she moved in. She was that sort of person." Mrs Todd had left it to the children to call her what they liked, "she didn't want us to feel we had to call her anything and if we felt angry we could say 'Mrs Todd'."

Anne also liked "Dad" Todd especially, partly because "the men in my life up until then had not been particularly caring towards me. When he used to take us for walks, it was like going for a walk with a big brother. He was super, and one of the best things was, he used to muck about. If you wanted to sit and catch tadpoles, he would sit on the wall, kicking his legs and watch us, and join in the fun. I used to think that was great and when we were actually walking, we would go for miles with him, we'd be tearing about all over the road and everywhere, and I remember I used to hang close, you know, if I got the slightest chance I was holding his hand. I can remember that, and if anybody else got his hand I was madly jealous. He was very friendly in that way and I felt it was all right, I had a friend, not necessarily someone I could tell my troubles to, just a person in the background, like a big teddy, to run to for comfort."

When Anne and her brother were later placed with foster parents these two people of whom Anne was so fond strongly disagreed with the decision, but because they felt it would have been wrong professionally to tell her they never let her know this until after the foster home had broken down and she returned to see them as a young adult.

Sometimes a member of the domestic staff became a very special person, and was remembered with love years later. The photograph given to Andrew by the cook who was so kind to him has been mentioned elsewhere. He spoke of her often in the group discussions.

"She always seemed ever so interested in what I did and she always treated me as someone special. Whenever there were roast potatoes, she knew that I liked roast potatoes, and she would always make a point of saving a couple for me, and as soon as meals were finished I would creep into the kitchen and she would say 'I've got your roast potatoes on a plate in the larder' and I used to creep in and hide in the larder eating these roast potatoes. I really felt towards that woman, she was there every day, she was part of our life.''

''The fact that she'd thought of me every time, she'd be glad to see me every morning when she came to work, she'd always speak to me. It wasn't really necessary but she always did. She must have had some sort of attachment to me as a child, liked the look of me. Well, I must have been the same as every other child there, but I suppose she singled me out.''

Barry said, ''With me it wasn't the cook, it was the washer-up, I used to go to her house quite a lot on Saturdays.''

Although their experiences had been mixed, some members of the group were prepared to express the view that on the whole they had been lucky to have lived in the children's Homes they knew, but they were eager to discuss some of the implications of their experiences. Two had not only lived in residential care but had also worked in residential establishments for children since they went out of care. In addition some had experience of bringing up their children so that they had first-hand knowledge of their needs as well. They looked at the general issues of staffing ratios and deployment of staff from all these points of view.

Starting from the principle that children in care should be provided with adequate individual care and staff time, they considered that one person on duty with three children under five would be a minimum, but in more general terms they thought the numbers of staff provided should be related to the needs and problems of the children. For example, ''If they were handicapped children they would need many more members of staff than you would need to look after normal children.'' Leaving aside the problem of defining handicapped and normal, they were amazed to be told by one of the professional workers that ratios of care staff to children in some schools for the handicapped were at that time considerably lower than in children's Homes. From their own experience in children's Homes they underlined the need for individual attention as they saw it: ''You see when he goes to bed a child likes a story or something. When we went to bed there were perhaps twenty-five of us, they couldn't all sit with each one individually and read a story,'' said Andrew. ''We used to have to read stories to the little ones, and to bath them,'' said Margaret. ''I don't think this was good for the little ones because they needed a mother figure and we weren't that; we were more of an older sister and little ones need motherly love.'' She had found from working with children herself how poor staffing ratios are bad for staff as well as children. ''It must be awfully frustrating for the staff too to have so many children demanding and not being able to give this (that is, motherly love). I found this, so many things pulling you in different directions at once and you couldn't give your full attention to any of them.''

The way in which staff were organized was also seen to be of significance in the amount of individual attention each child received. The impression Andrew had of his last children's Home was that there was a very large group of children, about fifty or so, and only three care staff to look after them. Factually this was inaccurate. The number of children had been about twenty eight to thirty and there had been five or six care staff, a poor ratio but better than he remembered. Discussing this it emerged that because at that time the children were dealt with as one large group with all the care staff relating to them all, instead of as later with small groups each having its own staff, the feeling left was as Andrew described it. In fact he said, ''I would have done better to be born ten years later perhaps.''

Andrew felt it was important too to realise how differently a child perceived the scale of everything compared with an adult. The experience of returning as an adult to buildings which seemed very large when a child, and finding them quite small and ordinary, is a familiar one to most of us. The size of groups may have similar connotations, Andrew suggested; a group of fourteen for example, with one or two people looking after their interests ''seems something more gigantic to those fourteen than it does to an onlooker.''

Margaret's impression of her children's Home had been

similar. Staffing ratios were not high, but all the children (about eighteen to twenty) were at that time cared for in one large group. She had memories of a "vast amount of staff", "milling about doing their jobs", but not available to individual children. Referring again to the bathing of little ones in which she had participated, she said, "the adults would come in and say "All right" and go out again. There was no personal contact with those people and the jobs that you would normally do at home together, such as a member of staff washing up as well as the children, the children would wash up and the staff would be the overseer." As a result of large groups Andrew felt there always seemed to be, "not regimentation as such, but in the normal functions of the day there seemed to be this regimentation of breakfast in the morning and lunch. Everyone had it at the same time whereas probably in a smaller group with more individual attention there would be less emphasis on this. If you were an hour late having tea simply because you had been doing something it wouldn't matter. We all sort of got into a routine of things."

In the unhappy event of his own children having to be in care and having to go into a Home (rather than into foster homes which he believed he would prefer) he would want them to go into something "as near as possible like a small closeknit family rather than amongst a large number, or what seems to a child a large number. In my case twenty seemed a large number and being lost as it were." He envisaged, if such a Home were not available, a large Home should be broken down into smaller groups to give a child the "more natural" care he needed. He saw it in these terms: "He becomes a nonentity when he goes to school and is in a class of about thirty or forty; when he comes home he comes to his mother, father and perhaps another two children in the family. Whilst they are in care not only are they a nonentity at school which can't be avoided but when they come home it is the same. It is exactly like school in a lot of respects, and therefore they gradually lose the family atmosphere, it doesn't do anything to keep them closely knit."

Soon after Andrew, Margaret and Barry had left the children's Homes they lived in, the local authority had adopted a policy of small groups whithin all its homes, including its only residential nursery where tiny babies were included in groups of no more than six children of all ages up to seven or eight. This was contrary to the prevailing practice at the time of separating babies, "tweenies" and toddlers into age groups and moving children on to other establishments when they reached school age. The policy met with a certain reserve and caution from official visitors at first; but later became a recommended pattern. Margaret was unaware of this but had worked in a group of children's Homes in another area after she completed her training as a nursery nurse. In these Homes she said the toddlers and early school-age children were mixed but the babies and young children up to toddler age were separate. She recounted that some of the children used to say, "Why can't we have the babies with us? It would make us more of a family instead of having them up there (that is, in the nursery) because we'd love to look after them."

Official views do not always coincide with the feelings of consumers about the services they are offered. Elsewhere in this chapter it has been stated that the group of Homes which were inherited by the children's department in question were considered unsuitable and isolated. Pressure was exerted by the central government department to persuade the local authority to dispose of them and replace them with other accommodation, smaller, nearer to schools and employment and more likely to be absorbed into the surrounding communities. Three of the group who had lived in the cottage Homes saw them much less critically.

"You'd got swings, a big lawn, everything and yet you were still allowed to go out. There was plenty of light and it was fresh, a very nicely situated place, the river not far away and it's an ideal spot for children to live. OK, perhaps the schools are quite a way, but there's a school bus anyway." Another factor which they thought was in favour of these

Homes was that they provided opportunities for brothers and sisters to be together because they were large enough to do so, and this made for a family atmosphere. On the other hand when Barry was boarded out not very far away from the Homes, he found that people in the community whom he had expected would be against him because they were "against the Homes" proved to be quite easy to get on with and he realized "while we were in the Homes there definitely was a barrier. We never talked to anyone in the village."

The concept of community Homes which in 1970 was being promulgated as part of the philosophy of the Children and Young Persons Act, 1969, was greeted by the group with enthusiasm for certain aspects of it. It prompted them to emphasize the need they saw for flexibility of management in the interests of the children's needs. "You have got to get rid of regimentation, even down to the minute details. I think fixing a special day for visiting is one of the regimentations you have got today," said one member. Accommodation to allow parents to stay when visiting their children struck the group as just what was needed, and they saw that it might have the additional benefit of helping parents to talk to people about their problems. They made it clear, however, that they would hope the delicate balance in community Homes between being part of the community and maintaining privacy for children who saw the establishment as home for the time being would be preserved.

At the time that most of the group were in care official attitudes, training, child care policy generally were discouraging residential social workers from attempting to be substitute parents and encouraging what was believed to be a more professional approach to the task. The group members were unaware of this trend and were thus uninhibited by it in the emphasis which they gave to their own priorities. Buildings, equipment, opportunities to play and the general physical atmosphere of homes were important, but to them the attitudes of staff and the atmosphere they created were the essence of any establishment as they saw it. The staff who had twenty-four-hour a day responsibility for children, especially when those children were either without an effective parent or saw their parents relatively infrequently, had to respond to the child's basic human need for parenting or he remained deprived.

In the first couple of hours of meeting the opinion had been expressed by the group that "someone you could look to as a father" was needed in a children's Home. Later it was put as follows: "Isn't that person you call Auntie and Uncle the most important person in your life when you are in care? It's not your child care officer but it's that person that cooks for you and washes for you and all the rest of it." These were not the domestic staff though, as has been seen, they can play an important role, but these were the people who for the time being undertook the full-time care that children require. This care has to extend to the provision of real comfort and solace when these are needed. "Say the welfare officer (that is, social worker) has to come and criticise the child in some way, then it's got to have somebody to turn to and if that person is in the room it is very important, even if they just fling their arms around them and sob like hell, it's just to know that there is somebody else there." The care has also to extend to support in major crises, when residential staff are the only people a child or young person can turn to. One of the group had been working in an observation and assessment centre. He described how a boy on remand, being visited by his probation officer, might be buoyed up by his recommendation to the court that a probation order should be made. On the other hand the probation officer might come and say, "Sorry Tim, I'm afraid this time it's approved school" (that is, he would recommend this to the court). At this, "the poor kid's just split into a thousand fragments" — at this point he desperately needs the help of someone on the residential staff of the establishment.

Although in discussion of the role of field social workers the group commented on children's need for some physical contact with them, and although they assumed the nature of children is to need people who will hold them while they cry, or have a temper, as well as listen to them and make plans for them, they never at any time envisaged the field social workers playing the role they expected of residential staff in the examples above. Yet the rapidity with which many children try to make some relationship with people and places was exemplified in discussion of another observation and assessment centre (then known as a reception Home). "It's almost inevitable when a child first comes into care he has got to be assessed to some extent. It's OK saying 'this is just a little time gap while we assess the child', looking from the outside! The child already starts to make associations with his place and it becomes a part of his history, then he is moved away again and the poor kid is in another tizzy and doesn't know where he is."

Members of the group were not aware that this had been an organizational dilemma for the child care service since 1948, but their own feelings and experience and their knowledge of the feelings of many other children with whom they had lived while in care informed their comments. Their personal perceptions of the time they spent under observation and assessment are discussed in more detail in the following chapter.

6 Other Forms of Residential Care

Children's Homes had been the mainstay of the system of residential accommodation in which members of the group had found themselves whilst in care, but there were other establishments which some of them had experienced as well. Carol's and Miranda's involvement with residential nurseries has been mentioned earlier, but they were too young to have more than fleeting conscious memories of them. The reception Home (the kind of unit now known as an observation and assessment centre), and the hostels for adolescent boys and girls, were other parts of the system.

Six members of the group had been through a period of observation and assessment whilst accommodated at the reception Home.[1] Andrew and Derek were accommodated in children's Homes from the first day they were received into care and therefore had no special preliminary observation period. Alex was the one who talked most about the reception Home. Apart from a period in a residential community in another part of the country it was the only residential care he experienced because his father was able to provide for his holidays and his continuing interest was always available and dependable. Alex liked the reception Home, "there was a big garden and I liked messing about in that, and we did some camping. It wasn't exactly camping, but we had tents and things like that." There was also a smaller house in the grounds which for a time was used for older boys. Alex saw this in terms of something to look forward to, a kind of graduation point, but before that time was reached in his case he had left. Nevertheless, as he put it, "if it's a reception and assessment centre, they did a very good job because I didn't know they were assessing me." He also liked it "because it was a fairly structured place. I was told what to do, and if I didn't do what I was supposed to do, I got it." He confessed this was only an impression, "in fact the most I ever got was once being shouted at although I was there for eighteen months."

Barry had felt less sanguine than Alex about his stay there and could hardly remember anything about it except confusion and not knowing why things were happening. Although he was there with his older brothers he received little reassurance as a result of communications through them but suffered a great deal from the loss of his mother, removal from home, and as it appeared to him, an uncertain future.

Margaret's impression of the reception Home, her first placement on reception into care, was that it was enormous. (In fact it accommodated twenty-six to thirty children.) She had no idea how long she was there but she remembered being happy there. A specific incident shortly after she arrived, was a bonfire and fireworks for November 5th. Like Alex, she had no idea she was being observed and assessed.

Valerie lived in the reception Home for over three years until she moved on to the girls' hostel. In discussion she wanted to know why. The explanation she received would not sound out of date fifteen years later.

"One of the difficulties," said the children's officer, "is that having made your diagnosis of what the child needs it isn't always available, so the most flexible and accepting place is often the observation and assessment centre. They have got themselves geared to constant problems in a way that perhaps some long stay Homes haven't."

It had been difficult to decide what was best to help Valerie, but she had stayed there for the additional reasons that it was near her home, she was doing well in the local school and would have had to change schools again at fourteen or fifteen, a step which it was thought would have been unnecessarily disturbing as well as probably impracticable.

General discussion of observation and assessment led to consideration of using such centres for day visits. Group members found this proposition hard to accept even though they were assured that some children were assessed in this way and even asked to be able to attend on a daily basis. Barry said, "I'm quite sure I wouldn't have wanted to go in for a day to think that I was going to be observed to know where I was going to be sent to!" "They must be desperate," agreed Margaret.

Andrew shifted the discussion on a little. "Why not bring the whole family into a central help point? As well as (the children) having the company of the parents it would be avoiding in some cases a drastic split, and in other cases it may be the mending factor and they may then be able to go to a home centre, family centre or something, call it what you will, for a period, like someone who has been in hospital for an operation, like convalescence, to mend whatever it is that has broken and then to pick up the threads of life again." He saw the situation of some families as "an illness of a different kind, psychological or something like this." He thought this suggestion might in the end be less expensive than some alternative measures and would certainly be a better environment for the children. Pressed to pursue the practical issues involved if a family were able to leave their home for a period of perhaps a month he said, "I was going to come to that, I was going to say, make sure that the accommodation they leave is kept in the order that it should be, that is, rent paid and good upkeep in their absence so that they know that they are going back there, that it is something that is only temporary." (He was not aware that Derek's mother had been sent alone to a rehabilitation centre for neglectful mothers from which she returned to find her husband and herself homeless. At least partly in consequence of this the family had broken up permanently.)

Andrew and Margaret discussed his proposal.

"There is only a certain sort of person that one could help like this, those that really want to be helped, those that are really concerned about their children," said Margaret. "When they have got to the point where they have called in the local authority," agreed Andrew. "But very often they don't do this. It is an outsider that calls in the help," Margaret replied. "Oh yes," said Andrew, "but they have got to the point where lurking in the back of their mind they know that they might have to part with the child or that their family will have to break up. I suppose a lot of us who have been in care, our parents must have reached this sort of point, where they realized themselves that it wasn't a good thing, or that it was a disadvantage to the child perhaps, or was unfair to the child that they weren't able to give (him) what they should, perhaps emotionally or in some other way; obviously they must have got to that sort of point to have let us go into the Homes that they did." They continued to explore the practical issues:

"I think you would have to have plenty of these centres within close proximity of the husbands' work. Whether this would be a financial possibility or not I don't know," Andrew wondered. "They would have to be well known because people wouldn't be prepared to accept doing this unless they felt confident about them," Margaret responded.

Pursuing the idea of "an illness of a different kind, psychological or something like this" — Andrew went on, "You see the child might be taken away at the moment because the mother is having a nervous breakdown and even though she is on the verge of a nervous breakdown, this is detrimental to the child in that it is being parted from its family."

"This is the time," agreed Margaret, "that I think either makes or breaks the mother when a child is taken away from her. I think it is more important that they are kept close together."

"This is one of the cases where moving lock, stock and

barrel to a centre could be the answer, could cure the nerve trouble and also keep the family together,'' said Andrew.

Valerie had experienced separation from her eldest child, both when he was admitted to hospital and when she had her second child. ''Think of the poor children if the mother did go (that is, to hospital on her own). I know my little boy would go mad. He did when he went into hospital. I was lucky enough to stay quite near him but he used to break his heart every time I left him. It got to the stage where I hated to go to visit him because it would upset him, but if I had been with him it would have been all right.''

''In the very special circumstances that we are talking about you wouldn't be visiting, you would be there all the time so this wouldn't even come up,'' Andrew replied.

''I was thinking about Christopher when I went into hospital to have Candy,'' said Margaret. ''I used to telephone him in the morning and he used to phone me in the afternoon and he used to come and see me every evening and it would have been better if I could have had the baby at home but they wouldn't let me; but he used to break his heart even though he had a lot of contact with me.''

''When I had Kevin last year Mark went to my mother-in-law,'' Valerie continued, ''and nobody could do anything with him, not even my husband, and he was staying with him. And I was in hospital for a fortnight and he went mad. He didn't believe it when I came home. I hadn't seen him or spoken to him because the children weren't allowed up (to visit). I think it hurts the mother as well as the child.''

''Would everyone agree that there is perhaps less of a stigma from everyone's point of view in moving lock, stock and barrel with your family to a centre than there is in splitting up the family and taking them (the children) away?'' Andrew asked.

''Yes, I think there is,'' replied Margaret, ''because you could always say that you were going for a holiday; no-one need know where you were really going.''

''You could say you were convalescing, anything,''

Andrew agreed. "When you come back after an illness you go away to rest and then you come back to start life anew, and I think this would create the same impression, that you were going somewhere to sort out problems and even get marriage guidance, see how other families are coping under similar circumstances, how they are being sorted out, because I think a lot of children's problems are mainly the parents' problems and inherited from the parents."

Barry also agreed. "I think the sort of system where the family is moved to a centre, then I think the local authority could take the decision better, even better than they could within the observation centres, as to what happens to the child from there."

"The problems are not only the child's, they are the parents' too," Andrew repeated, "and in some cases you would observe just the child in an observation centre and not observe the whole picture."

The four adults involved in the discussion quoted above knew how it felt to be separated from their own parents, but three also knew what it felt like to be a parent. They were clearly more interested in considering how separation could be avoided than the merits and characteristics of a children's observation and assessment centre. In addition they thought observation likely to be more effective if the child were with his family than in a strange setting on his own, when they considered the picture would be incomplete. One of the features of the future community Homes' scheme which had attracted them when it was described was the possibility of the Homes being far more flexible, far more part of the community than some of the Homes in the past. Some of them felt parents would properly be more involved in these Homes, though they were realistic enough to envisage some of the problems that might arise in consequence. Their experience suggested there would be some children whose parents did not come to see them feeling left out, some parents who would be in and out every day of the week, and friction between staff and parents because of emotional conflicts on both sides. If parents were to stay overnight they would need proper accommodation, they might need to be enabled to join in the life of the establishment with their children and staff would need "to be trained in family case work and not just (with) children."

"They need to be able to talk to an adult and not have all those emotional feelings towards a mother or father, as the case may be, that has perhaps ill-treated their child, and yet the parent doesn't think they have. They may have been ill or something and they haven't realized what they are doing, and it must be so easy to say 'Oh, just keep your eye on that parent and make sure they don't do this, that or the other to the children.' Being a parent knowing that you were being watched and you are not sure what for, would be an awful sensation. It would be terribly difficult for the staff."

Thus compared with the importance of the long-stay children's Homes experiences, the observation and assessment centre had more significance in the discussions for the ideas it prompted about dealing with whole families at crisis point than for what it achieved or how it affected individual children. The theoretical background was politely accepted.[2] The reality for the members of the group was that the periods they stayed were much longer than would have been necessary for observation and assessment, they did not know they were being observed and assessed, nor whether what happened was what was considered right for them or not. Did it matter by comparison with family shame and distress at the hard facts of being found inadequate and having to be split up? These feelings showed through in the discussion above when the group was considering how to explain the family's departure to a centre, "You could always say that you were going for a holiday, no-one need know where you were really going." "You could say you were convalescing."

Similarly differences between one sort of service and another which administrative boundaries and legal and financial constraints impose on the thinking of those working in the services meant little to them in terms of human need. The separation of mother and child by hospital care had similar connotations to other separations experienced in the context of personal social services. The main difference perhaps was that no one need feel ashamed of being ill, so that complication did not arise.

Facilities for observation and assessment were new and additional measures required by the Children Act, 1948, to improve child care services for those who needed them. Hostels for working boys and girls on the other hand in some local authorities had been provided by the Public Assistance committees. The Children Act, 1948, included this power and made it clear that young people up to twenty-one years of age, or beyond in certain instances, whether in care or not, could be accommodated.[3] The local authority in question opened two hostels, one for girls in the nineteen-fifties and one for boys in the sixties. The girls' hostel was originally able to accommodate twelve girls, but later when an extension was built on, numbers were increased to fifteen. Two of the group had lived there during the time when it was changing from one group of twelve to several smaller groups, one of which was centred on the bedsitters which with their own kitchen and bathroom formed part of the new extension.

Valerie was there when there was still only one group and after the life of the observation and assessment centre, she found it "more orderly". "You had to do your fair share of everything and I think if I'd stayed at home I would probably (have) run away, or got into other trouble. I probably wouldn't have gone out to work, I'd have taken days off and spent my money instead of saving it. I think everyone respected Auntie Mary when I was there, there was no favouritism at all."

Carol had been there later. She had jointly occupied a gabled top room with another girl, "the top attic room; the funny-shaped room. It's a lovely room." Then she had returned during a time when the hostel group was in a temporary building awaiting the completion of the bedsitter wing and subsequently had been an occupant of one of the new bedsitters. Although a lot of thought had been put into the concept and plan of the bed-sitters extension, reality was inevitably affected by the way the staff managed the situation and the limitations of the building which were only discovered in the use of it. It is rare for the clients of social services to be consulted about the planning of buildings; it may not always be practicable, but certainly their experience and views could be helpful in the monitoring of the effectiveness of buildings. At the time the extension was built there were no other similar units from which experience could have been drawn and a number of practical difficulties were not fully anticipated. Carol pointed out that it was not much help having bedsitters so that girls could work towards independence and entertain friends if they were not allowed to entertain friends because there was no separate sitting room and guests were not able to be entertained in the bedsitters! In discussion it was explained that hers' and others' experience and comments had led to changes which met the problems they identified to a considerable extent. There was no doubt that those members of the group who had lived in the hostel had found it helpful and supportive at an important stage in their growing up.

Three group members experienced forms of residential care outside the facilities of the local authority; one of these was a boarding school, one a residential community from which the older children went out to school; the third was a psychiatric unit in a hospital. The use of each of these had been decided after very careful thought and in consultation with parents in two out of the three cases. The experiences which resulted were said by the group members concerned to be satisfactory in two cases and a great mistake in the third. These judgments were made in spite of both the "satisfactory" experiences having contained much that was disliked and resented at the time.

The unsatisfactory experience was the boarding school, although the school was one approved by the central government department concerned and was used extensively by other local authority children's departments. Miranda, the group member concerned, having experienced many difficulties in coping with day education, had been asked by her social worker whether she would like to go to a boarding school. She described her reaction as follows:

"Well, there was me with my 'School Friend' comics and 'Girl' comics, and you know, you always had a story about a crowd of girls at a boarding school and you imagine something like midnight feasts every night and swimming at midnight and all this sort of thing. So I said I'd like to go. But it wasn't until I got there and mixed with the girls that I realised they were all from broken homes, or the parents couldn't look after them. They weren't there for the education anyway. In fact the standard of education was very low. It was really strict; it was so strict that it was unbelievable. If you spoke in the corridor you were given a black star which was bad; if you were really naughty, like coming in late for dinner, you got a black mark, which was three of the black stars, and if you were caught nicking the strawberries like I was, and apples, you got a conduct star, and that was five! And naturally I was always getting conduct stars. After about five of those which was twenty-five black stars, you were sort of bawled out in front of your House and everybody picked you to pieces and of course, you'd stand there defiant with your socks hanging down, your dress all dirty, and big holes, things like this, and they just pulled you to pieces and put you on Coventry which I thought was too ridiculous to be true. They used to send you up to the top of the building; it was an old house, and I'm not kidding you, there (were) bats in the roof. I used to be terrified up there. But I went up there so often that I got used to it."

Miranda was very unhappy at the boarding school and each holiday begged, sometimes stormed, to be allowed to leave. "Every term I went back and was a bag of miseries for the first month and I could never whole-heartedly enjoy myself there no matter how much I tried. They changed headmistresses in the last year I was there. And it went from one extreme to the other. When I say strict, it was so strict you would think you were in another world, and this next woman, she was so lenient. You had girls walking out of the school at midnight, meeting boys in the village and things like this. I wasn't one of them because I was a senior then, so I had to be careful what I did!"

The school was closed soon after these events and Miranda had her wish, but she did not forget and the group meetings gave her the opportunity, as described earlier, to say that she should have been believed when she complained!

Another group member, obviously shaken by the stories Miranda told, asked if the school was "cased" before she was sent there. It had been fully investigated by all normal means, but as group members themselves had pointed out, it is not always possible to tell what the quality of life in a residential establishment is like unless it is lived in for at least a short time. Miranda might not have found it easy to fit into any boarding school, but she had great spirit and a good deal of sensitivity as one of her many stories about her school demonstrates:

"We used to entertain the Evergreen Club once a year in the summer term and we enjoyed that because it was old people who didn't get out and about very much and it was a real pleasure to have them. And I had this same old lady three years running. In fact I still write to her. I remember the last time I was there when they came, I picked a rose for her and told her to take it home to remind her of when she came up here. And do you know, the trouble I had just because I picked that rose. You just wouldn't — it was unbelievable — well I just laughed in the headmistress' face. I thought it was so funny, and of course, that made it worse, the fact that I laughed. I just wouldn't believe her! But I could understand from the point of view that if everybody picked a rose for the old ladies there wouldn't be a garden left, but they had plenty of garden there!"

Miranda had not much she could give! She was only

allowed 1/6 pocket money a week while at school, even though the rest of what she was entitled to as a child in care was saved for her to have in her school holidays at The Beeches.

Alex, who on balance thought his placement in a residential community had been of benefit to him, nevertheless saw what Miranda meant about "boarding school" and had experienced one housemaster who had come from a boarding school. This man was not liked because:

"There was a terrible sort of clique atmosphere, all his friends (were those) who liked being organized, and the one or two who didn't like it really got it from him. They hated him and consequently there was a direct confrontation because they didn't want to go and play football so they wouldn't, and so there would be a regular sort of punch up and he would end up with the big authoritarian touch, hitting the boy and demoralising and humiliating him in front of the others."

Alex enjoyed a good deal about the establishment but he objected to the pressure put on him. He thought the Gordonstoun type of philosophy, "Nietzschean" he called it, was held in high esteem by some of the staff, but he objected to it and did not wish to become a "superman". However he valued the sense of belonging which he gradually acquired and spoke very nostalgically of the times he had spent there and the people he knew. He had met an ex-school friend in the train one day and talked of how much they both enjoyed exchanging notes about mutual experiences and acquaintances. He told the group he was going to a reunion, an event which took place about every two or three years. "It's a reunion that's very sociable. I think this is something that children's Homes miss. The first thing is old members of staff are still there — or some are. You have, of course, to regress, and you are a boy again, and it's great fun. It makes me have some form of completeness, you know. I wouldn't turn to it in times of great need or anything like that, but I think it should be something that everyone can turn to, some sort of memory of a happy childhood, or a childhood of adventure, mucking about." He went on to contrast the way in which staff in children's Homes "have a tendency to get up and leave after two years," whereas in his residential community some of the staff had been there most of their lives. The establishment also had what Alex called "an ethic". He felt that the structural identity which came from this was missing in most children's Homes even when children lived in them for a long time. Another member of the group contrasted the satisfaction Alex was feeling about this "reunion" with the fragmentation of life in children's Homes. Even if an ex-child in care called back, as he had, and even if the staff he knew were still in the children's Home, the most he could hope for would be some information about other people whom he had known who might also have been back to visit, but otherwise "once you go into the outside world as it were, you never see each other again."

Finally, one member of the group had experienced in-patient care as an adolescent in a psychiatric secure unit. She had not considered herself to be ill but receiving treatment for a behaviour problem and was in no doubt, six years later, that the treatment had been effective. She did not regret having had it, although it had involved some potentially threatening and some unpleasant experiences. "It wasn't very nice, but it was worth it in the end," she said, having described the treatment to the other group members. The doctor was someone she trusted. "He really was a good doctor and seemed to help most people who went (there). He was a fatherly kind of man, I could talk to him, he was quite reassuring to talk to." But the treatment was received in a setting of which she was very critical and in circumstances which she thought should have been better managed. The reasons why the treatment might help her had been discussed with her at the time when entry to the hospital was being considered and she had been prepared for the idea of going. However, because of the circumstances of demand and use of the hospital's beds, she could not be told when she would go and when the time came it was at very short notice. In addition, because of the nature of the treatment and the impossibility of forecasting the time required for it to be effective, she had not been able to be told how long she would be in the hospital. Initially a period of about six weeks had been discussed, but in the event it was eight months before she was able to be discharged. During that time on several occasions she had weekends out but it was a long time particularly as she was in "a locked hospital and there were girls from borstals there as well, which I didn't really think was right. But there again, I suppose he was a busy doctor and you just have to take what comes." She had been able to work in a sewing room in the grounds, but "when I thought I was coming home I went mad. Eight months seems an awful long time when you're locked up, because not even the windows opened, apart from a few inches, of course. I suppose they had to be careful because there were so many girls there from borstals and remand Homes. But I was thrilled to think that I was coming home, fresh air and daylight again." Looking back Valerie had no doubt that if she had been the social worker in charge of her case, she would have made the same decision, but she regretted the physical constraints of the secure unit, the hospital clothes, the lack of baths, infrequent changes of underwear and having to be with people suffering from a variety of conditions from epilepsy to severe physical and mental handicaps. Other members of the group questioned why this had to be so and were told that provision for adolescents in need of psychiatric in-patient care and treatment was very scarce and considerably less than was required.

Between them the group had experienced a wide range of types of care and establishments. Their perceptions of staff and staff relationships were keen and clear, though inevitably they remembered best what affected their day-to-day life and how it felt, rather than understanding fully the intentions and policy which lay behind the methods and events they experienced. They understood that they themselves presented problems; on the other hand they felt that a number of their problems were unnecessarily created or increased by rigidity in staff attitudes, unwillingness to listen to explanations and too much uniformity in the handling of individuals. What remained with them and was treasured was the kindly, patient understanding that made some staff stop and listen, try to help them sort out their tangles and problems and come to terms with life as it seemed to them. The firm, but gentle, member of staff was seen as "the best of the lot" — and was the one who only had to ask and they got up and did what she wanted.

7 Fostering and Adoption

The Curtis Committee, whose report led to the setting up of local authority children's departments, placed great emphasis on foster home care. They saw it as the preferred method, after adoption, of providing a substitute for a child "deprived of a normal home life" with his own parents.

"Adoption is a method of home-finding specially appropriate to the child who has finally lost his own parents by death, desertion, or their misconduct, and in a secondary degree to the illegitimate child whose mother is unable or unwilling to maintain him. If it is successful it is the most completely satisfactory method of providing a substitute home."[1]

"We have placed boarding out next because of the view expressed in nearly all quarters that it is on the whole the best method short of adoption of providing the child with a substitute for his own home.[2] . . . . . far more children could be boarded out if there were suitable homes for them."[3]

Before 1948 two different legal codes had governed practice concerning boarding out by the local authorities. Education departments in the main held responsibility for children committed by juvenile courts to the care of local authorities on fit person orders and were required to board them out with foster parents, or to provide the government department concerned, the Home Office, with an explanation for their failure to do so. Public assistance departments, on the other hand, who cared for the homeless, destitute, abandoned, deserted, orphans and others received into care with the consent of, or in the absence of, their parents, were under no such obligation and although some children were boarded out, a high proportion lived in the residential Homes about which the Curtis Committee were so critical. There many of them suffered the institutional practices and deprivation which distressed the committee and helped to reinforce their preference for the more "natural" conditions of foster homes and adoptive homes. Adoption, they knew, could not be widely used because the consent of the children's parents was required and was unlikely to be given in more than a very small proportion of cases. Fostering did not involve breaking parental ties, however, and could therefore be used more extensively.

The Children Act, 1948, gave legislative support to the Curtis Committee's emphasis on fostering by making it clear that it must be considered first for every child received into care. Only "where it is not practicable or desirable for the time being to make arrangements for boarding out"[4] was the local authority free to maintain a child in its children's Homes or those provided by another local authority or voluntary organisation.

The effect of this was to put very considerable pressure on local authorities to use boarding out placements in foster homes as a means of providing for children in care, rather than residential Homes. The Children's Inspectorate of the Home Office in the early years after children's departments were first established made regular inquiries in local authorities to ascertain how many of the children in care were boarded out and, where the proportions were low, urged increases in field work staff and energy to be invested in finding foster parents. A number of residential Homes were closed in consequence and for some years there was considerable emphasis on "boarding out percentages" of the total numbers of children in care. These were sometimes seen as a measure of good child care.

As they explained, the Curtis Committee's strong emphasis on adoption and boarding out had been based on the opinions expressed in evidence to them, and on their own observations of children in foster homes in twenty areas in England and Wales. What they saw impressed them; "most of the children were living the kind of lives which they would have lived as true children of the home,"[5] and "the contrast between the children in Homes and the boarded out children was most marked. The boarded out children suffered less from segregation, starvation for affection and lack of independence. They bore a different stamp of developing personality, and despite occasional misfits were manifestly more independent. For example, they were much more indifferent to visitors, were much better satisfied by their environment (by which we mean the special features of security and love). There was, we thought, much greater happiness for the child integrated by boarding out into a family of normal size in a normal home."[6] Some of the evidence they received was expert, for example the evidence of Dr Donald Winnicott and Dr John Bowlby, but little specific research or consumer reaction studies were available at the time they were reporting or when the subsequent legislation was drafted. It was only after boarding out had been given such prominence that major research studies began to be carried out[7] and experience began to demonstrate that, like other forms of substitute care, the use of foster homes was only suitable for some children, and at some times, not necessarily for all or in all circumstances. Thus when further changes in the law were made in 1969,[8] fostering lost its legally supported priority and took its place beside the range of residential care facilities as part of the spectrum of methods needed to provide for children in care, the preferred method for any individual to be chosen according to his ascertained need at the time.

The local authority children's department responsible for the care of the group members, like other children's departments, passed through various stages in its development of a spectrum of methods of care, including the use of foster homes. In the first few years after 1948, there had been great enthusiasm and pressure to board out and this had resulted in decisions such as those which affected Martin and Derek, that is, to separate some children from their siblings on the grounds that they could more readily be found foster homes and would benefit from them more than remaining in residential care together. In Martin's case he had been the baby in a large family; in Derek's he was the child that prospective foster parents always found attractive while his little sister, though equally attractive in appearance, was unhappy, fretful and disappointing by comparison. Similarly Carol, a child whose unmarried mother could not provide for her, seemed an obvious choice for boarding out, with the hope that later if her mother agreed she might be adopted.

Barry, as one of a family, some of whom grew up and left the children's Homes when they left school, also seemed likely to benefit from fostering. Miranda, unlike the others, had been privately placed by her parents in three successive foster homes between the age of about three and four and a half. When she was received into care a second time, the decision was made to keep her in a residential placement, young though she was, to protect her from the inevitable upheavals created by her warring parents in any situation where professional training and support were not available to cope with them. Andrew had almost reached school leaving age before the pressure to find foster homes began but he was required to go into lodgings when he left the boys' service in the armed forces because local authority policy at the time did not allow working boys and girls to live in children's Homes. Valerie and Alex were never considered for fostering because of the circumstances of their individual needs and Margaret, although after much careful thought she was boarded out, never really settled and did not regard the experience as satisfactory either at the time or later.

Group members thus had considerable experience to draw on in discussing fostering as a method of substitute care. In addition seven of them had experience of living in lodgings. Because they were relatively young and lived with the families there were thus similarities to the foster home situation, though there were also significant differences due to the different financial and contractual relationships which existed. Two members also had experience of being adopted and although both adoptions had been largely unsuccessful in the eyes of the adopted persons, their experiences were of great interest in the general context of the discussions.

Martin had had the longest boarding-out placement in the group, virtually the whole of his life. He had no memories of residential care because he was placed in a foster home at a few months old and had been there ever since. Listening to others talking about being in residential care, and the need for individual attention which each child feels, prompted him to join in the following exchange:

One group member said "It is individual attention that makes you feel you can get through to someone, doesn't it? You can't do it when you are a load of people together. You can't make contact with one person."

Martin replied, "No, you are sharing and you might see them once a day, you might see them at bedtime, and that's it for the rest of the day. Or in the morning when you get up you might see them (that is, residential staff). But when you are fostered out you see them in the morning, noon and night sort of thing. It is totally different, I should think, in a Home, pushed and shoved and moved around like this. Those who are fostered out, I should think, from my experiences, have had the better time of it than those who were in the Homes."

Andrew, who as a working boy was not allowed to return to his former children's home when his short career in one of the boys' services ended, saw the lodgings he was found as a kind of foster home but wondered why he had been placed there. "Although I didn't make a success of it (that is, the boys' service) and although it hurt my pride rather to think that possibly I'd be going back there (that is, the children's Home) I would have loved to have gone back rather than gone to a totally strange (place).

"When I was allotted foster parents I was allotted an old lady of about seventy and to a boy of fifteen with no other people in the house at all, she was totally out of touch with me as a youth. I wonder whether the people in charge of me realized I was very unsettled. I seemed to get the impression that possibly they didn't because of the fact that I was shipped out to an older woman." He spoke of "Fate taking a hand" — "and it was only on personal contact with a chap who lived in the house behind who was getting married to this local girl, when she vacated her parent's house and they got married, that she had the kindness through the friendship with me to say, 'Would you like my room with my parents? My parents have got a boy, he's the same age as you are; I'm sure you'd like that. Would you like that?' and I fixed this up privately and went there and lived there and left the old woman, and although I am very fond of the old woman, obviously it wasn't a good thing for me as a youth at that time because there was no common interest." In fact the children's department had been involved and supported the move, but the initiative had been taken by Andrew and his friends. He and this family had become close friends and "they are virtually like a mother and father to me now."

Andrew thought when a boy or girl left a children's Home to go into lodgings they needed "to go into a family atmosphere. I think from the age of fifteen to eighteen is a very important phase in your life when you are being thrown out, well not literally thrown out, but you are being pushed out into getting a job and on your own, you've got to start standing on your own feet and there isn't anyone. Suddenly you say "Oh my goodness what am I going to do?"

In the discussions about residential care the group had suggested that it was very difficult for anyone to know what a Home was really like and what happened in it, unless they spent at least a short period living in it themselves. The children's officer asked them whether they thought it was possible for people outside of foster homes to know what they were like for the children who lived in them. One member was prepared to say "They don't." She continued, "Well, you get the child care officer coming to see you and the family as a whole. They always listen to the mother or the father. They might listen to the child but they wouldn't take any notice of what they say, and the mother just says the good things unless you've been really bad and she has a good moan. But somebody coming from the outside can't really tell your proper position there." When asked how the child care officer could make opportunities to talk to a foster child alone, the group member replied, "Well, with my Mum you can't because she always wants to be the main person that's talking." This group member claimed there had been many things she would have liked to be able to talk about to someone outside the foster home but that she did not have the opportunity because she thought she would cause offence to her foster family if she tried to do so.

On the other hand another member recalled that she "was left on my own to talk to my child care officer when I was in the first foster home." Her foster mother would say "Well, you talk to Miss Brown while I go and make a cup of tea," and she always gave me the opportunity to do it."

A further member said his experience was that he never had an opportunity to talk on his own. "Often I wasn't there anyway (when the social worker called). If I was there we just talked together. I don't think my foster people would have liked to push us into another room to talk on our own. She (the foster mother) was rather domineering and she would want to know what was going on. Not that I minded anyway. I didn't have very much to moan about so things were all right."

Derek wanted to know if "foster parents are given a certain number of rules" before they take a child, and an explanation of the Boarding Out Regulations and the form of undertaking signed by the foster parents[9] was given. The delicate issues of how foster parents and foster children have to relate in a situation in which someone from a local authority or voluntary organization has to supervise were discussed. Group members could see that both children and foster parents needed someone to talk to but that the "secret relationship" that is, the one in which they might each be talking separately to the third person, was a difficult relationship for all concerned to manage. One member had bitterly resented foster parents telling a social worker about a diary she had been keeping. Another member thought it was possible that foster parents could "get rather frightened and don't know quite what to do." "Isn't there a situation where all the foster parents and adoptive parents in a certain area get together and discuss their problems?" asked Derek.

"I wonder what the foster children would think was going on," said Carol. "They needn't know," replied Derek. "But why shouldn't they know? The relationship is a big thing between everyone concerned, and trust, and we can't get trust if things are going on secretly behind your back. It has got to be spoken about openly," said another member.

"If there were an older child, couldn't they go with the parents?" Carol suggested. "No, that would defeat its purpose then," said someone else.

Martin had earlier said that if foster parents accept a child as their own that child wants to live in the same atmosphere as the family, squabbles and all. On the other hand the public nature of fostering could create problems as it had in Derek's foster home.

"Most people have neighbours. One day I had quite a quarrel (with the foster parents) and the following week one of the welfare officers came and said that the next-door neighbours had written and complained that I had been ill-treated, and that hurt all of us, that one of the next-door neighbours had written to the council."

Nevertheless the need to safeguard children who may be suffering without being able to talk to anyone was accepted. A few children, like one described by a professional member in the group, desperately need an outside person to discover their unhappiness and prevent further harm coming to them. She described "a small boy who was fostered with a family, and I took it on as a going concern. In fact I hadn't been supervising it very long when this child picked up a ten shilling note, I didn't know anything about it until I was asked to move him, just like that; he had been there several years, but he was a thief! He had found ten bob and had spent it! Investigating it I found that he was sent to bed because he might affect their own children. For about a week when he wasn't at school he was in bed. I then went to the school to talk about it and they said, 'What could you expect of that sort of child, he pinched.' The foster parents had been to the school. I had had no idea of what was going on, and he wasn't allowed to get out of bed to talk to me. He used to just weep and weep because he didn't know what he had done wrong. He needed someone to talk to and I hadn't asked the right questions and the previous person hadn't asked the right questions. The child knew he was unhappy; the foster parents knew that they weren't treating him the same as their own children. How does the person from the outside find this out?''

The possible role of teachers in this context was discussed but it was recognized that to be able to help, teachers may need not only to be sympathetic and understanding but also to have access to information and to be knowledgeable about children in need of care and some of the risks which may affect them.

Some of the stresses which foster children or adopted children suffer in certain circumstances may be of the local authority's own making, even if this is unintentional. The local authority concerned had developed a policy of short-stay fostering and also multiple foster placements, sometimes of whole families of children, sometimes of several children together in one home. The following is an impression of a foster home taking several children of different ages and with various problems. The foster mother in question was a widow with a daughter of her own living with her. She was regarded by social workers as being very adaptable and willing to take children in emergencies. This is how it seemed to one consumer. "I think I liked being in the children's Homes more than anything because nobody belonged to anybody. When these Homes closed down I hadn't quite finished school so I went to stay with a Mrs Henderson at Waterton and she seemed to have thousands of people in there. Freddie Smith came there first of all with me. I don't remember what happened to Freddie, he was there one day, and he wasn't the next. Where he went to I've no idea, I didn't even know he was going. There were thousands of people and everyone belonging to everyone else, except for the little girl called Monica. There was a daughter (of the foster mother's) who had got a hole in her heart or something, and this little one had been fostered for her sake. It was very complicated and I can't remember it all." The facts of this foster home and the placements of the children in it looked very different seen from the official end of the telescope, but this was how it was remembered by someone who was fifteen years old at the time.

The residual extra-sensitivity, separateness and aloneness of a child or young person in care even in relatively favourable circumstances can be seen in the next memory contributed by Andrew as a result of Margaret discussing the problem of being locked out by her foster mother when she came home late from the local youth club. She had had a boy friend who would have climbed up and opened her bedroom window so that she could get in but she had felt that she shouldn't have been locked out and had said, "Well, I'll sit on the gate until she will open the door! And I just used to sit there."

Andrew responded to this. He had previously warmly described the life-long friendship which had developed between him and the people he went to live with after he left his very elderly foster mother, but nevertheless he had had a painful experience with them once. He had been out "with other boys, youth club activities or something, and it was rather late, or I may perhaps have been courting and they threatened 'if you come in late we'll lock that door' you know and 'we want to go to bed' and I did get home late, and all the doors were locked. I remember I just turned round and walked out of the place and went back to the friends that I'd been with and said 'I've been locked out' and their mother put me up for the night and breakfast. I had a spanking breakfast in the morning and do you know, I went back about mid-morning and those people struck me as being very frightened that I'd done that.''

One of the most painful contributions made by a member of the group illustrated the way in which being in care may often mean that a gain is counterweighted by a loss, and how easily a child's grief can be misinterpreted. After a number of introductory visits to their prospective foster home the day came for Anne and her brother to leave the children's Home where she had become very attached to the members of staff and to go permanently to the foster home.

"I remember looking back at the doorway of Bluebell Cottage with Sally and Neil (Todd) and Auntie there and all the kids, and even thinking about it now brings a lump to my throat, but at the time I cried, like a dog does in the throat, and I didn't want the Fletchers (the foster parents) to see. I didn't want them to feel that I was ungrateful, but really, with all my heart I wished I wasn't going. I suppose I was very quiet on that journey. They must have thought I was being rebellious or something but I couldn't say anything, didn't want to. It was a sort of whiney feeling in my throat and I didn't want to express myself in any way and I was like that for quite a few weeks after I arrived at the Fletchers. I knew there was a wall being built up and even then, when I was eleven, the Christmas probably before my twelfth birthday, I think they made reports that I wasn't easy to get on with because they told me this; they knew I was a sulky child and all this. I knew I was as well. But when I first went to them I wasn't being sulky, I was living in a state of remorse. I suppose I had got so used to the habit of looking back on life that I never really got out of it, and that's true for the whole time I was there, for six years I think it was.''

Another group member responded:

"You talk so vividly now, I wonder whether perhaps you could have talked to anybody as you are talking now?" Anne replied that she could not have talked to anyone she knew at the time. She had not known, because of their sense of professional integrity, that the residential staff to whom she was so attached had strongly opposed this particular foster placement. "I didn't know but something told me they didn't want me to go. It's a sort of sense, isn't it? You sense these things. I think children are very perceptive. I think that Sally (Todd) really did feel that we'd lose out in some way; because the Fletchers were so cool. They had me for six years and I can't honestly see why they fostered me in the first place. The only reason I can think of for them wanting to foster me was in the beginning perhaps they wanted children, but I think after that it became more of a status symbol they wanted. They wanted a good couple of youngsters who got on well in life and they could say with pride, 'We've brought these two up, look what fine youngsters they are.' They made such a fuss of things. You couldn't do anything really without a fuss being made about it, even the washing up. We had to do the washing up, well that was no hardship, but when it came to, well you know what kids are, my brother and me were always fighting. I can never remember a time when we weren't fighting, except when we ganged up together against them, on these little country walks we took. We walked for miles, the two of us, and we were being fostered, taking them apart, putting them together again with ogres' heads on and all sorts of things. But apart from that we were always fighting and in the kitchen when we were doing the dishes, we used, if we weren't fighting or bickering, we were at the other extreme, laughing and carrying on, you know. Its only natural I suppose, but as soon as the laughter started, it was 'You'll break something, stop mucking around!' In the end we were apart. We are very apart now, my brother and me. There's a sort of, I don't know, a very wide gap between us."

Anne was asked what she thought was wrong with the

choice of foster parents. She replied:

"Well, I don't think, to be quite honest, I'd have been blissfully happy with anybody because I can remember my mother so vividly and anybody who deliberately steps out to take her place or gives me that impression immediately turns on a feeling of hate automatically."

"So you shouldn't have been fostered?" asked the children's officer.

"Well, I wouldn't say that," Anne replied, "but for somebody to say 'Well, I'm not your Auntie Elspeth anymore, I'm Mum now, you can call me Mum!' That to me — I didn't like that. It was different calling Sally (Todd) Mum because I made up my own mind about that, there was no hard and fast rule, 'I'm not your Auntie, I'm your Mum now'. I accepted her (Sally) without question."

Miranda, who had lived in a children's Home and boarding school for most of her life, had a number of adjustments to make when she first went into digs. "I wanted to be like a working girl, be with a family, leave a family in the morning, this sort of thing. I suppose with me being completely out of everybody's way (that is, away from the Home where everyone knew her) starting off clean and a new job, new home, chance to earn money and buy my own clothes, it sort of went to my head. That's when I first started going into pubs and going out with boys. They (the family in her digs) couldn't understand why I wouldn't take a boy home and in fact I was there nearly a year and I only took one boy home. Fortunately it was one they liked. But I could never talk to her (the wife) as an adult would talk to an adult."

Miranda resented being asked questions about where she was going, when she would be going, who she was going with and always answered "Don't know". She realized later that this was quite a normal pattern on both sides, but at the time she thought the family in her lodgings were being "nosey". She was also puzzled by other things.

"Things like washing up, she'd get all ratty if I didn't offer to wipe up. I mean, now I just do it automatically. Washing up at The Beeches was a lot different from a small house. You used to take it in turns at The Beeches whereas in a small household I'd be doing it every meal. This sort of thing just didn't strike me as essential when I first went there; I just didn't think of doing it. I didn't offer because I didn't want to do it, but I just didn't think of it."

Carol who had been placed as a toddler in a foster home and adopted later had suffered the confusion and threat of other short-stay children coming and going and not being very certain of her own status.

"There were all sorts of different people coming and bringing children and that, and they used to start asking me questions and saying 'Have you been good?' and 'How are you getting on at school?' and all this sort of thing. I used to think that everybody could come and push me around. It used to get on my nerves a bit." She remembered vaguely being adopted but never felt as much part of the family as her parents' own natural daughter. As the years went by she became more aware of her feelings and during adolescence, about school leaving time, a crisis developed which led to her leaving home and living for a time in the local authority's girls' hostel, later in digs and then sharing a houseboat with a friend. Looking back she had felt that there were real injustices in the way she had been treated, and that the boys who were fostered in the same home were treated with much more flexibility. She had also resented what she saw as a demand for gratitude by her adoptive parents.

"When I was adolescent, my parents have always given me the impression that I owe them something, that they had me to do me a favour and I've got to give them something back. This is what annoys me because I wanted to be like other children, not have any responsibilities, and I still feel that I owe them something, but I don't know what."

However, when pressed by one of the group — "Would you rather you had no ties at all? You'd like to be independent would you?", Carol replied, "Well it's nice to have them; I am independent but it's nice to know that there is somebody. I get on well with my sister (nine years older); it's nice to know you've some kind of family.'' Carol admitted, as Miranda had too, ''I always like my own way.''

On the other hand some of the experiences she recounted seemed to support her feelings of being discriminated against in favour of the younger boys. When she went home on visits after leaving to live elsewhere, unlike her parents' natural daughter she was expected to do cooking and other tasks for the whole house even if her visits were quite short. Yet when she tried to demonstrate her feelings for her parents they seemed unable to respond appropriately.

''Just after I got engaged, Mum and Dad couldn't come to the engagement party so Tony and I decided to cook a meal for the four of us at Mum's house. Well, we did it all out lovely, you know, candles and everything on the table and it came round to serving it up, I served it up and there were the boys sat watching television and I just said 'Why can't they go to bed and we can just have it, the four of us?' and they (her parents) turned round and said 'No'. They started giving all their food to the kids. They didn't just sit down and enjoy it. That upset me.''

Discussion in the group suggested that the staff of the children's department should have been more sensitive to the needs of an only girl in this household (the natural daughter being so many years older) and not place only boys, nor perhaps so many. It seemed an example of an over-willing foster home being over-used. Carol also felt that the boys who were fostered were able to feel more secure than she because they had been placed as babies and had never known anything else but their foster home. In addition she felt she could have weathered the flow of short stay foster children if it had not begun until she was old enough to understand and not be threatened by it, for example, at thirteen or fourteen years old, ''but all through my life it's been children staying and going. If ever I said anything to Mum about it, I can remember saying 'you always give more attention to the baby of the family than you do to the others,' and she would say 'well, you don't need it as much as they do.' But you do! You need just as much attention as a small baby does when you're about nine or ten, because its at the time of life when you need to feel secure. Because Mum's attention has always been on smaller babies in the family she really hasn't had a lot of time for us when we were growing up.'' Carol thought her mother was one of those who always needed a baby. ''As soon as one starts school she's lost and she doesn't know what to do so she's got to have another one. Then as soon as that starts school she's got to have some more and so on. She's never been able to be just on her own at home. She keeps saying 'I'm not going to have any more when these have gone' but she just wouldn't be able to live without a baby in the house.''

The problem of the conflict between the need of a local authority for foster homes and the needs of the foster parents' own children was highlighted by this discussion.

Derek's view of fostering was very similar to Martin's in some respects, but since he was older when he was placed his adaptation had been more conscious. He had missed his little sister and retained a sense of responsibility for her which he had not been able to act on until they were both adults. He had been brought up in a ''near adoption'' situation and referred to his status in the family as ''adopted''. He used the same words as Martin: ''I was just one of the lucky ones.'' ''I was adopted,'' he continued. ''They said they came to pick one out, just like a market or something, and I turned round and smiled at them and that was the deciding factor; and I feel it was a partnership, not so much they were doing me a favour, I was doing them a favour as well. She couldn't have any more children, I think. However, I didn't hear anything more about that, that's what I assumed anyway. So we were both doing each other a favour. I treated them as my real parents, always have done, and, as I say, I was just lucky.''

Derek's placement had happened during a time when methods and procedures in the selection of foster parents were not very fully developed and it was not always easy to persuade staff, committees or members of the public that it was not desirable for children to be selected for placement by prospective adopters or foster parents coming to see them in a group. Derek could recall his early impressions of this at the children's Home: "I remember looking through the door and thinking 'surveyors!' They used to become sort of commonplace, nobody used to take any notice of them when they came."

"And who were these people?" asked the children's officer.

"Prospective adopters and things like that," he replied.

Derek told the group he thought his sister should have had the opportunity to be boarded out or adopted rather than him, because "it matters more to a girl having a stable home, doesn't it?" At the time the group was meeting he was trying to help his sister but finding it very difficult because of the long gap in their relationship and the lack of common experience. "It's a new game to me, that big brother bit. I go round there and every time I try and sow the seeds I'm accused of lecturing; that shuts me up."

Barry felt his foster home had helped him educationally as he explained when the group was talking about the effect on their progress in school of being in a group at a children's Home. In his children's Home there had been a television. His foster home only had a wireless set and the family used to read quiz books and do other things which encouraged him to make progress. In addition his foster parents had had a grandson who was "really brainy" and went to a grammar school. "He studied a lot right from the time he was eleven, so if he was studying and I'd probably got nothing else to do, I probably did some studying."

Andrew, who was very conscious of his lost educational opportunities, wondered whether a foster home would have helped him to take more advantage of school and all it represented. Derek thought it probably would have done and explained why:

"Well, I think that when you are in a foster home you've

got the parents there, the people acting as parents. They try to explain the advantages of studying at school and everything and you're encouraged then to study well, if not for the advantages, just to please them really. Whereas in a Home I suppose you haven't got anybody personal to explain these advantages so you don't really bother. You've got no-one to really please individually, that is. When you're in a foster home you study hard mainly just to please the foster mother.''

Martin supported this from his experience though he felt he might have done better. ''They looked after me as their own, sort of thing, and they gave me all the encouragement they could. Whether I took it was up to me. I was a fool that way, I was more interested in the land; to get out was the main object.''

Although Derek had such strong feelings about his sister's needs, he told his fellow group members he was very glad he had been fostered. ''I don't know how I would have managed if I'd stayed in a Home. I suppose I would have managed to fight on somehow, but it's given me a more secure background, being adopted. I was pretty proud of it. I felt different from the rest of the class. I remember walking out with my head held high for about a week, the fact that I'd been chosen. I did miss the other kids for about a week then I forgot about it, I had so many other things to occupy myself.'' He thought children should be placed very young in fostering or adoptive homes ''so that they can adapt straight away and then make it permanent.''

At the time the group members were discussing fostering, there had been a nationally publicised ''tug-of-love'' case between a foster home and the natural mother and some of them wanted to talk about it.

''I've got views on that,'' said Derek. ''In the paper recently the mother's claiming them (her children) back just because of something written on a bit of paper. I think this is wrong; once they've settled in somewhere they ought to be allowed to stay. Its bound to disturb somebody isn't it?''

"I think to have had the real mother going to visit the child and forming an association with the child would have been better than trying to get the child to go and live with her," Margaret replied. "To suddenly want the child back, to suddenly go and put the child with her when this other woman had given the child everything . . . She (the foster mother) had been with this child twenty-four hours a day and then just to go to somebody else . . . . !"

"Perhaps she (the child) should have been boarded out with somebody else apart from both and allowed to make the decision for herself," said Derek.

"Then you are going to tear a child three ways instead of two ways," protested Martin. No-one in the group held the view that the natural parent's rights should be supported against the child's interests.

In the context of discussing the problems which lead to children needing substitute care, one of the members asked:

"If a child goes into care, does it automatically go into a Home? Could it not go to foster parents?" When the reply confirmed that this was one of the possible ways of providing for admission to care, the members with children of their own all expressed a preference for foster homes in the event of their own children needing care. The view was also expressed that children who had no parents should have priority in being found foster homes. Gradually the group began to develop the idea of a kind of travelling foster parent, not a home help, not exactly a social worker, but someone who could work with the family and help to prevent the children having to be removed from home, though they recognized that a point might be reached with some families and some children where the home situation could not be contained by these measures and "then we get back to the point of foster mothers," said Valerie. She felt there might be some children who could not be controlled by foster mothers any more than by their own mothers and that these children might need "a stronger hand altogether."

"But all they want is somebody who really cares," said

Margaret, "not somebody who is going to be an authoritarian person because they would rebel even more against this."

"Possibly the average foster parent isn't even equipped to think in these terms anyway," said Andrew. "They perhaps only think initially about providing a child with a home and catering for its day-to-day wants, and don't think that it goes very much further than that."

Barry asked: "The ordinary foster parent doesn't really have any training, do they, but if it was someone who had worked in the (children's) department or worked with children . . . .?" and the idea of training foster parents emerged. Margaret took it up, saying, "But then as most foster parents have already got children how are they going to have their training because they can't be away during the day time with their own children?"

"You could have courses where they could take their children with them, like during the summer holidays. How long does it really take to train someone?" asked someone else.

"You could try to instil into them a knowledge of children," suggested Valerie.

"Perhaps it would be a good idea for them to go and live in a children's Home and let their children see what it is like as well," Margaret added.

She asked Barry if when he made his suggestion he had been thinking of people who would be prepared to train as foster parents. He said he had been thinking more in terms of people who had worked for a children's department and because they were well known to the department could be selected more easily for this type of work. Speaking of possible incentives for such work, Margaret thought "people might do it for the satisfaction of seeing a child happy perhaps." Andrew thought they should have a financial satisfaction as well: "It is getting to the stage where doctors, nurses, teachers, all sorts of people, the responsibilities that they are coping with are far outreaching the monetary rewards that they get. I don't necessarily think that all the while you should think that you have to be paid for what you do, but I think it should be catered for nevertheless. It shouldn't be just shelved as 'Oh, they are volunteering', or that 'They have taken this training, therefore we can shove the most difficult child on to them'." He felt that "perhaps there are a lot of unknown individuals who would take on the job today if it were not for the conditions that exist."

The question of whether children were affected by the fact that people were paid to look after them brought further experience from members of the group of when they were in foster homes. Barry said, "I don't think a child naturally thinks of money being paid to look after him. I think it is only in moments of anger, when they want to get back at you, when they throw this up at you in the hopes that it is going to anger you. I certainly wasn't conscious with my foster parents that they were being paid to look after me." Margaret said she was aware of it but acknowledged that this may have been because she did not like the foster home anyway. Miranda's view was that foster parents already pay "rates and taxes, why should they pay more for the rest of us." Derek wanted to know whether foster parents could "be incorporated in these councils (that is, local authority councils) to give an idea of how much it would cost." He thought it was "usually people with no experience at all with the general costs of bringing up children who were involved." Perhaps with his own foster parents in mind, who would have liked to adopt him but did not feel able to manage without the boarding-out allowance, Martin also wanted to know whether children who were legally adopted were still financially assisted by the local authority.

The selection of foster parents and adopters was a problem which prompted many questions from members of the group. Many of these were to obtain information about the methods used by the local authority and the reasons why certain procedures were used. Others were based on their own experience or related to cases of foster children about whom there had been publicity in national newspapers. Derek was reassured to know that adoption societies were regulated by law and another member of the group was speaking for them all when he said, "The deeper they delve into the lives of the people who adopt the better it is for the children. I don't think you should take any chances."

8 Field Social Work

The post-war changes in local government social services for children included not only those which led to different patterns of organization and responsibility, to materially improved and more sensitive residential establishments, and greatly increased use of fostering as a form of substitute care, but also to the emergence of an important group of professional staff, field social workers. Before 1948 there had been a few workers in local authority services who were in some senses forerunners of this development but there was no specific training for them and they were few in numbers. Work concerned with children committed to the care of local authorites was often carried out by staff of the education departments, supervision of privately fostered children and children placed for adoption by health visitors, and children in the care of public assistance committees by public assistance officers or members of their staff. On the other hand sometimes responsibilities were combined and carried out by the staff of one department on behalf of the others, or in some instances, members of the committees shared visiting responsibilities with staff.[1] There was no equivalent of the post-1948 field social workers, known variously at the beginning of the child care service as boarding-out officers or visitors, children's welfare officers, child care officers and other similar names, but eventually known nationally as child care officers.

The Curtis Committee report had attached great importance to the development of a personal social service carried out through staff who had knowledge of individual children and acting on behalf of the local authorities as a friend and supporter to each child in care.

The committal of the child to the care of a Council which takes over parental rights and duties is not without incongruity. To be properly exercised the responsibility must be delegated to an individual and that individual one whose training has fitted her for child care and whose whole attention is given to it.[2]

Although the child was committed to the authority,

The Children's Officer would be the *person* to whom the child would look as guardian.[3] We attach great importance to establishing and maintaining a continuing personal relation between the child deprived of a home and the official of the local authority responsible for looking after him . . . It will not be practicable for the Children's Officer of a large County Council or County Borough Council to know and keep in personal touch with all the children under her care, and she should, therefore, aim at allocating a group of children definitely to each of her subordinates. The subordinate officer would, subject to accidents, illness, change of employment, and the incidence of retirement, be the friend of those particular children through their childhood and adolescence up to the age of sixteen or eighteen as the case might be."[4]

The Curtis Committee believed training of field and residential care staff to be an essential element in bringing about the changes they considered essential, and even before the Children Act, 1948 was passed or had begun to be implemented a few pilot training courses had been set up in universities and the first students selected for them. The memorandum on training which the Committee submitted in advance of its main report envisaged for field social workers a pattern of theoretical and practical training in child development, family life, social conditions, social services and the agencies through which they were rendered, and assumed that members of the enlarged Government Inspectorate relating to the child care service would also take training where necessary.

In spite, however, of this emphasis on an informed and disciplined approach to the important task of helping children "deprived of a normal home life," the numbers of persons trained on courses for the first ten years or more remained small compared with the demand from local authority children's departments and voluntary agencies who also needed trained staff.

Even by the early 1960s the number of child care officers completing training each year was still much less than was needed particularly in view of the expansion of the child care service which was greater and faster than the Curtis Committee had envisaged.

The inevitable corollary of this was that many staff were untrained, though some of them were experienced or qualified in other professional disciplines, for example, teaching or health visiting.

The enthusiasm and aspirations of the new service nevertheless meant that individuals increased their knowledge and shared experiences through the means of professional associations, publications, regular discussions and debate in the professional forum. A strong sense of identity existed within the service and there was a widely shared desire to achieve implementation of the objectives set by the new legislation. These were accompanied by awareness of the need for better standards of care generally, for more sensitive handling of individual children and for a commitment to their needs which would take precedence over many other considerations.

Nevertheless, as the experience of the group demonstrated, public attitudes were slower to change and administrative and official constraints of many kinds affected the type and quality of service given. Individual differences in staff attitudes or performance also produced their own constraints and problems and were of considerable significance to the children and their families who received the service.

Some of the differences between residential establishments and their staff and between individual foster parents and adopters have already been seen through the eyes of the group members who had spent years in their care. By comparison field social workers spent comparatively little time with each child for whom they were responsible. In spite of this their role was of great significance because they were involved in some way in every stage of a child's life while in local authority care. They investigated referrals of families needing help, they were involved in deciding whether or not to receive children into care, where to place them initially and where they should next receive substitute care. They had contact with juvenile courts, with the children's schools, doctors and other services as well as parents, relatives, prospective foster parents, adopters, lodgings and places of employment.

If special opportunities offered or disasters occurred, the field social worker was involved; he or she was likely to be the person who arranged transport or took a child on to his next destination, or escorted him on some occasions at least to hospitals, further education establishments, and job seeking. The social worker visited the child in his children's Home or foster home and it was his responsibility to keep the child in touch with his family whenever possible. In addition much of the record of decisions, placements and events depended on the field social worker's reports written in a variety of circumstances and for a wide range of purposes. The field social worker was, in fact, the most important link between the many people and organizations with an interest in or responsibility for a child in care.

Although members of the group when they were children in care themselves had been ignorant of many facets of their field social worker's role and responsibilities, and even by the time they met together as adults were still mystified by much that had happened, they clearly recognized the influence that social workers could have and saw them as important people in the settings in which they had found themselves. Early on in the discussions one member had put forward the idea that the social worker should be a "bridge" for the child between one set of adults and another. Another saw social workers as necessary "because children in care, they're on their own, aren't they?" to which a third responded, "They're completely on their own and they need that outside person, somebody else coming about and everybody else in the children's Home accepts this, that there is somebody else."

Their experiences of individual field social workers had varied as much as their experiences of residential staff and foster homes. "I remember I always felt that the child care officer was a rather distant figure to me," said Alex. "He didn't really inform me of what was going on. I suppose it depends upon the child, some children don't really mind. I was the sort of person who liked to know where I was going and what people were actually doing to me, even to the extent that it was under the Children's Act, 1942, or whatever it was, you know. He did insist on coming down and saying 'How's your school report?' and I didn't really care how my school report was in the least. I wanted to go out and have a nice cup of coffee in some really sleazy coffee bar and be shown a man's world! He had a rather nice car and I wanted him to go off tanking down the M1 at about 140 mph, sort of thing. I didn't look at him as a father figure, I looked at him as a person of interest and he never really fulfilled that, so I wasn't very interested in him in the end." Later Alex had another child care officer who "would talk about his family to me. He ran a little Morris 1000. He nearly drove me round the bend when he drove me once to the Midlands. He's the worst driver in the world and I was trembling with fear as he would overtake, but somehow I established a much firmer relationship with Mr White than I did with Mr Gray because he seemed to be much more interested in me. I liked him because he was a much simpler sort of man and he was willing to say 'I'm wrong', sort of thing. We would go into a coffee bar and he would say 'Look at these outrageous prices' and I'd agree with him."

Margaret responded: "I had a very good relationship with my child care officer and I can remember on numerous occasions going out with her, say to fetes, or out for the day and things like this." She described one of these occasions when she had won a doll in a raffle, and her child care officer was as thrilled as she was about this. "We had tea before we went back to the children's Home and I remember going back and not minding a bit. I didn't like the children's Home but the fact that Miss Brown had taken me out and we had been somewhere different made it all the more bearable to know that there was somebody outside."

Margaret, in fact, had had two child care officers with whom she got on well. "They are really more like aunts than anything. I usually called them Auntie."

"I think it's very hard," said Miranda, "to strike a good relationship with a child in care because I used to look towards a child care officer as somebody from the office who was having a good old pry. Obviously now I'm older I realize different." Someone else said "Well, Mr Jones was one of the best blokes I've ever known, I think. I got on very well with him but I didn't see a lot of him though, that was the only trouble. He used to come about once a month I think. He used to take me home and bring me back at weekends from Bellevue House, and when I went to my training course I used to see him less than ever then. He was the sort of person you could look to and ask him anything and I could get through to him. It was more like a fatherly understanding because I never had a father."

Andrew asked the group, "Did you get the impression as I did that the times that you did see a child care officer was when you possibly had to be fitted out with a new outfit or something like this and you were taken on a trip to an outfitter. It was an important event in your life, you were changing schools or something, and then the child care officer came and saw you and you went somewhere with her. Other than this you didn't perhaps have any personal contact."

Because he had been in care earlier than any of the rest of the group, he had only had a child care officer in his last few years in care, at a time when a handful of people were having to carry all the field work of the department. He was concerned that there should be more contact between children and their social workers than he had experienced: "The child care officer was just a shadow in my mind, I don't even remember a face," he said.

Barry had also been received into care during a time when there were only a few child care officers, and when old practices were dying hard. "As far as I can remember we were at school, my mother had died a few weeks beforehand, we were at school and this lady, I can't remember her name, just came and picked us up and we were whisked off to The Cedars. Whether she told us or someone else told us that we were going away for a fortnight's holiday to give my father a chance or not, when the fortnight was up, and I actually counted the days and thought 'Good, it's time to go home,' and then I was told 'No you are not going home, you are staying a little bit longer.' I can't remember who told us this but that was the bit at the time which hurt me most."

As the years went by the local authority in question built up a qualified staff of field social workers who tried very hard to achieve good standards of work in their contacts with the children. Because caseloads became smaller they were able to spend more time on individual cases and to carry out more thorough investigations, supervision and general casework.

Sometimes this resulted in individual problems being very promptly sorted out to the child's satisfaction as when Margaret was very upset about an incident in her foster home. "I ran to my mother. I didn't know where I was going. I had a bicycle and I got on it and cycled from Westfield to Torton. I don't even know how I got there!" When she arrived someone telephoned her child care officer who came immediately and said, "Now what's it all about?" "I can remember her saying that, 'What's it all about? Why did you do it?' I just burst into tears and said, Well I'm not going to be called a liar, I'm not!' I was so het up about it, I don't know why. I wanted to get away from that place. So I said to her, 'Well, I'm not going back there, I won't go back for anyone,' and she said 'Yes you will, you will go back there and stay at least tonight and I will come and see you in the morning and we will talk about it then when you have calmed down,' which she did. She was back virtually after breakfast the next morning and she talked about it. What had been decided I don't remember, but within a few days of that I had left that place and I was happy about that.''

Anne did not feel so positive. Her child care officer took a great deal of trouble and spent many hours with her and her brother and with the people concerned with them. Yet when she was asked whether she felt she got to know the child care officer during that time, Anne said, ''No. The other welfare officers who came weren't so well-dressed. She was always impeccably well-dressed and that made her seem a little more austere to me. She seemed from a different class of people; I don't think she could possibly understand what I was going through. When I tried to explain she had these theories of her own which she more or less stuck to. If I said that I didn't like the Fletchers (the prospective foster parents), she would say that was probably because it wasn't a very successful day, something like that. I meant I *didn't* like them! I wouldn't say she wasn't listening, I would say more she was trying to understand me, but she wasn't trying to understand *me*, if you know what I mean. She wanted so much for it to go right, I know she badly wanted us to be fixed up properly. I know she was quite fond of us in her way, but to me it was a funny sort of fondness; it was as though we were godchildren rather than nieces and nephews, you know what I mean? Something that little bit further removed.''

Anne's next experience of ''welfare officers'' was when she and her brother were abroad with her foster parents in a country where there were no parallel services to those in Great Britain. The statutory supervision required for a foster home had to be carried out by a voluntary organization which provided general welfare services. The representatives who visited were described by Anne as ''nursing sisters coming round to see people like us and well, they hadn't really much interest. They were interested in little babies, expectant mums, so we didn't get much joy out of them. As far as us kids were concerned we didn't have anybody to turn to." Anne's foster mother, on return to England, had confided in a social worker that she too had longed to talk to someone and had not found what she needed in these international arrangements for supervision.

Anne had previously explained how she resented anyone who tried to take the place of her mother and one of the group asked whether she had ever been able to take anybody into her confidence about this. She said she had, a "very good welfare officer in Loamshire. She was the beginning, really, for me for explaining things. She really showed me how (I could) trust the child care officers. She brought things out into the open. She explained things to me that I hadn't had explained by any other welfare officer and asked my opinion and I thought the world of her just for doing that one simple thing, asking my opinion. I felt as though I had something to say, and why shouldn't I say what I felt, and when she asked me how I felt about things sometimes I used to be so overwhelmed I used to feel a gush of love for her, that she should know so much about me that she knew how badly I wanted to communicate."

Anne had not been able to communicate with the child care officer who had found her foster parents, and she also described a man whom she said "was a write-off. He was youngish, he couldn't have been more than thirty anyway. He had all these theories, more or less like Myra Brandish only she was more experienced. He had this thing about authority and discipline, a help as far as my foster parents were concerned! He was very fond of giving advice. 'You really mustn't let Anne get away with saying these things' instead of saying 'Well, why don't you think, the lot of you, about what you are saying, and talk it over instead of growing up all individually.' He had no idea. He really wasn't very much help at all."

Part of the problem for the social worker and the organization which supports him is that some of the events of life with which children in care have to grapple are of such dimensions in terms of shock, loss and long-term consequences that the resources of time and skill available are grotesquely inadequate, like trying to deal with the need for surgery by using first aid dressings or home nursing. Anne's experiences had been as damaging as anyone's in the group. Her mother's desertion had left a lifelong wound; the loss of her little half-sister was another major grief. The social worker and the organization had both expended comparatively intensive effort and comparatively large amounts of time trying to help Anne and her brother as a pair and also to find her missing mother and half-sister. Eventually the little girl was found and visits between the children were arranged, but by then circumstances and life had moved on and a continuing relationship of more than a tenuous kind was difficult to achieve. The foster home choice, in spite of the care and time expended, had been a mistake. The children's department and the child care officer saw their involvement in Anne's welfare as considerable, but to her life in the foster home seemed disastrous and her only gain in relation to her sister was two brief meetings. It would have been difficult for her as a child to have been involved in all the thinking and work put into the searches for her missing relatives and the organization of even those two brief meetings. In the choice of the foster home a combination of her belief that she should do what she thought would help her brother and the difficulties of communication between the children and their social worker were significant factors which helped to produce a disastrous decision.

Two members of the group told Anne how vividly she had communicated with them. She was able to put into words what some of them had also tried to express about their feelings concerning this important relationship of child and social worker.

"When you have a welfare officer as a child and you're not

really struck by them, every time I got a new one, then I felt 'I must be careful what I say. I don't know how this person's going to take it.' I was assessing them as much as they were assessing me really. I don't know how the others feel about this but if you've got a welfare officer appointed to you and if you don't happen to be able to get on with this person, or maybe just to communicate with them very well, what can you, a child, do about it? I mean, if you are in the kind of home, institution or whatever, where you haven't really got anybody in your confidence and your welfare officer is a bit beyond your reach, who can you talk to?''

Someone suggested a child should be allowed to change his or her social worker: "Ah yes," said Anne, "that's the crux of it all, not everybody would do that though." Instead, "They all disappeared and somebody new came and it was a new story, from the beginning. I got sick of telling my life story over and over again and not getting anywhere. It was very frustrating, whereas if somebody had said to me, 'Well, it's not that we think we can do nothing for you, it's just that this other person knows a bit more, and you might like them better than me,' or something like that. And you would perhaps have been able to communicate more freely. That's how I feel anyway.''

Valerie expressed the view that she never got any "straight answers" from her child care officer, "the issue always seemed to be evaded," although in many respects she thought she was very, very good. For example, when Valerie went into hospital her child care officer went to visit her at a considerable distance once a month, or every six weeks, and "if I wanted anything I used to have to write and ask her and she'd send it for me." The child care officer also wrote to Valerie every week and always kept her fully informed about any plans for her which were being made in the children's department. Yet Valerie had not felt it was any use complaining to her child care officer about conditions in the hospital because she had no confidence there was anything she could do about the situation.

"People don't take an awful lot of notice of children do they?" The relative importance of what was happening in family relationships compared with what the child care officer was contributing was also made evident by the fact that Valerie could not remember whether her worker went to court with her or not, whereas she remembered vividly and bitterly how her mother rejected her in the presence of the magistrates and the others.

There was no doubt in some group members' minds that the relationship between children and their social workers should be significant and close. "I know that you've got dangers of emotional involvement and all this sort of thing, and it is something that can't be avoided in certain cases, but the welfare officer's contact with the child should be more close; try and put yourself in their shoes, and say 'Well, how would I feel?' It's very difficult to be able to do this, I think. In some cases its virtually impossible but I think that all the time you've got to try and do it."

On the other hand two group members who had been long-term foster children, perhaps partly because they had wanted to feel their security was unthreatened by people from outside the foster home, partly because their foster homes had been the centre and focus of their childhood, saw field social workers as people who came from time to time to make sure all was well but not much more than that, though they recognized the potential for help was there if it was needed.

"They were just somebody I had to tidy myself up for," said Derek. "I don't know how often they came to see me. I never used to confide in them about anything. Well, I never used to tell anybody my problems, but I suppose if I had been of that nature where I confided in anybody I would have confided in them. They did their job well but I felt it was just a bit of routine when they came down, like an annual medical or something; that was the only contact I had. If they had come more often I would have been able to talk to them and when I got talking to them perhaps a lot of things would have come out. They were a sort of go-between (with Linda, his sister). If it hadn't been for them I wouldn't have got in contact with her."

Carol stressed how important it was, in her opinion, for a child or young person to be able to get in contact independently with a social worker. She resented the way her adoptive parents would get in touch with the social worker unknown to her and thus have opportunities to tell their side of the story behind her back. She wished she had been able to telephone the social worker without having to say everything in front of her family. Derek asked, "Couldn't the child care officer come right out when the parents and child are there and tell them an address where the child can write if he has any problems? Then everybody would know about it. Wouldn't it be better to bring it out in the open?"

"All this behind the back makes the child even more sure that they will try to get at the adults," said Carol, "and it doesn't help the relationship."

Miranda also felt that complaints about children should be made more openly so that the children had an opportunity to put their side of the case. "There was one occasion I really hated them (the people with whom she was lodging)," she said, "When they brought you out," (turning to a professional member of the group), "and told you about my diary. I think that was despicable. They could have spoken to me about it on my own and listened to me, and then informed you if necessary, but no, they went straight to you."

"Don't you think it is because foster parents get rather frightened and don't know quite what to do?" said Margaret.

It is not easy for those who provide services to retain their sensitivity to the recipients' perceptions of them and it is easy to forget that the user of a service may be seeing the service giver as someone whose terms of reference he cannot easily assess, whose power and influence he may assume to be considerable but not clearly defined, and whose reasons for action and decisions may be obscure. When the client is a child or young person there is the additional factor that the service giver belongs to the adult world which is still unfamiliar territory and relatively unpredictable in many of its manifestations. Furthermore, for the child or young person in need of care the adult world he has known is likely to have proved comparatively unreliable and unsupportive even in the best of circumstances. In the worst it may have been harsh, cruel, neglectful, disastrous to his well-being and safety and destructive of his confidence.

It is not surprising therefore if the adults who are providing a service have to spend considerable time and give massive reassurance to establish a relationship of confidence with him. In the case of field social workers the time for familiarization with the personalities and attitudes of staff which residential work affords is not available to the child. Encounters which to the field worker have provided time for a full investigation of a referral of need, a discussion with the child about his situation and what may be done to help him, a visit to a foster home or a children's Home, to the child are still only a few hours. During these he may be a silent observer of a discussion between adults, sometimes there may be a talk between him and the social worker, but they are a brief period only during which his anxiety is likely to make full concentration and understanding more difficult and therefore leave many questions and doubts unsettled in spite of the worker's best efforts.

This problem was discussed by the group in various contexts. One of the professional members of the group described a girl of fourteen with whom she had worked who never seemed able to confide in her or use her help although she knew that complaints about her behaviour were being made to the social worker. Only when she was in her twenties was this girl able to say, "Well, I couldn't see any point in talking to you then because mother knows how to deal with people and who would believe me?"

One group member responded that she sometimes trusted her child care officer and sometimes did not. Barry, who had described his experience of being received into care very abruptly and how he was told that he was going away for a short holiday only to learn, when he had counted the days to his return, that he would not be going home after all, described his child care officer as "very nice" and recognized years later that there were circumstances which helped to explain the apparently insensitive way in which his need had been met. However, he found it impossible to forget and his capacity to confide in or respond to adults who were providing him with a service was severely damaged at the time. Twenty years later he wanted to know whether a child of eight (his age at the time) "would now be told a bit more about what was going on." All he could remember was that "someone came to school, I think we were in the playground, and she recognized me and said 'Barry' to me, and the next thing I can remember we were whipped off. It might not have been like that but in my mind it's like that. This is the only thing I can remember that really terrified me."

The effects of shock and anxiety on memory and perception can be considerable. Discussion in the group provided vivid examples of this, particularly since some members had been children with whom one of the professional members in the group had worked. It was thus possible to relate their respective memories. These had been so sharply different in one instance that the professional member had referred back to records to check her own memory. Records had shown that she had spent much time in explanation, preparation and continuing support. Nevertheless the trauma the children had endured had distorted the whole picture and left only a feeling of being in the hands of unpredictable power.

The members of the group appreciated that their own circumstances and reactions to them made communication with adults difficult, but they also expressed in their own way some of the problems of formal interview situations with children. Discussing the possible value of going over a painful experience with a child after it has happened so that explanations and interpretation could take place, Margaret said, "I think if I had been told to sit down and ask questions

I would have gone completely blank and sat there like a doll. I wouldn't have known what to do. The only time I got any answers to any questions was Mrs Thacker (in her children's Home) saying that I was in care until I was eighteen, and I wouldn't be going back home. I just exploded and she exploded but I think that cleared the air for me more than anything and put things in a more realistic light.''

In general Margaret had warm feelings about field workers who had helped her, nevertheless she had this to say: "I felt my child care officers were inadequate. There seemed to be a lack of emotion. I felt that they were never quite with us, there never seemed to be an understanding between us." Martin, however, had had one of the same social workers as Margaret and had found her quite different. "She showed a great deal of affection rather than those other people who I've had from when she left. Perhaps it was because I was smaller then and younger, but she showed more for me than the others have. They come in and sit down and talk and ask you questions but they didn't give me the impression that they were interested, not really interested." Asked how they thought their social workers should have behaved, Margaret replied, "To have lost her temper with me I should think on some occasion that I was silly. My child care officers were too easy-going. If they had been a lot firmer I would perhaps have been less . . .?" Understanding was wanted, but firmness too. "I wouldn't have admitted it then but I admit it now; if she had been firmer we would probably have got on," said Miranda about her social worker.

Derek responded, "When a person loses her temper they (the child) realize how they are really involved in their case, but for a younger child I think it wants somebody who doesn't lose their temper." He was never angry himself when the fieldworker came to visit: "I never used to talk to them really, just sit there and be looked at while they were thinking and discussing me. I suppose if I was angry at any time I wouldn't like them to start off at me or reprimand me or anything; just let me know that he had taken note of everything and written it down in his book. That would make me feel better but I wouldn't like him to spout off at me." He explained that he would be reassured by having the field worker write things down because "then I would have known he had taken it somewhere else to be dealt with."

How could children be helped to understand what was happening in their lives? Weekly meetings in children's Homes when a senior member of staff would be available and children could ask anything they liked was one suggestion, but whatever method was used it needed to be recognized that children were unlikely to be able to grasp the whole situation at one time.

"They can be prepared before and told afterwards. The need to be explained to right up until it's happening and then after its happened, they need to be told and given the opportunity of asking," said one member. But this presupposed an element of continuity. "How can you give a child an emotional hand they can hold on to if, for instance, you don't hear about it (the event) until the same day? They don't get to know the person who is going to take them or anything, and nine times out of ten a parent can't go with them." She described vividly the feeling a child may have in these circumstances, a feeling which may make memory blot out part of the experience and make ears deaf to things which are being said: "Fear gives you a blind which you pull and it's just impossible to pull it back up again."

The group members had referred to changing faces and changing places as distressing. "People are so restless that they want to move on," said Margaret about child care officers in general. Another member suggested that each field worker should have a sort of community-based "deputy" who "wouldn't keep moving around as often as a child care officer and the child would probably get to know them." They drew parallels with some of the non-resident Homes staff they had known to whom they could go and just sit and chat, play with the cat, spend time with a companionable, dependable older person. There was some discussion too of the pros and cons of field social workers taking children into their own homes on short visits, as a way of helping the children to see them as people. One member suggested that it was important for the social workers to find out what interests their children had and then to try to share them. They might even take a short course in the practical things that children enjoyed doing. On balance it was clear that as the group members saw it from their own experience, good listeners, practical, understanding people who did not move around too often and whom they saw frequently were to be preferred. They needed to be people who could really share in the child's experience and convey their concern clearly to him over a significant period of time.

The group had regretted the number of changes of child care officers, yet some who had been in care for more than ten years had had relatively few changes because the department worked on a principle of not changing child care officers and cases except when officers moved elsewhere or were promoted internally. Considerable pressure had been exerted on the department in the interests of organizational tidiness and economy to change a child's social worker when he moved from the local authority in question to another local authority or within the area of the local authority when administrative convenience might have reduced travelling time and mileage. This had been strongly resisted by the children's officer, but at the time the group was meeting there were indications of further pressure to yield to administrative convenience and economy as a result of an organization and methods study. The group were asked to comment further on how they had felt about changes of social workers, and from their own experience how they would view an increase in such changes. They were critical of the proposal on behalf of both children and staff. Anne had moved about with her foster parents a great deal, in and out of England. Her experience suggested "if you have a system where you have a different person every place you go, if you were unfortunate enough to go to a lot of different places, I don't really think you'd get anywhere." As it was, "I had to give my own experiences to each person separately and I thought this was unsettling because I got so frustrated. I always felt I was saying the same thing so often, it was coming almost off a tape recorder. It's like the *News of the World.* When your feelings are become so well known you don't feel a person any more. You lose your sense of identity, I think."

"The child care officer wouldn't feel as effective or there wouldn't be the feeling of someone to turn to, or an authority who could do something for you. If they were changing so often you'd think, well, in another couple of months I shall be talking to somebody else and I shall have to start all over again," said another group member. Asked to comment on how they felt about a child care officer they had time to get to know, they said, "There is a feeling of somebody standing by you."

"Yes, I've got somebody there."

"Even if you don't get on with them very well."

"Yes, I've got somebody to talk to and lean on if anything does go drastically wrong. If I got to the state where I was thinking of committing suicide or something, you know, at least I've got somebody I could really turn to." The children's officer then asked them, "When you think about your life in care what does the child care officer stand for in your minds?"

"The in-between," said one.

"They are the translator between you and whoever it is that controls you at the office, or the head of the department," said another.

"When I was younger, I thought her job was official, like business. I didn't think she could be a friend anyway. They looked after my wellbeing but not so much my happiness."

"As you say, they were looking after your wellbeing, not so much you."

"Anybody unfortunate, I felt as though I was one of the unfortunates, and that they had a lot of people to look after on this caseload. I always felt that welfare officers, as I used to call them, were always more official than they needed to have been. They didn't mean to be, obviously. Although I felt my welfare officer wasn't a friend, I felt a lot better having the same person each time.''

The importance of the feeling of continuity was underlined by Margaret. ''I know in the back of my mind that if I was desperate about anything, no matter where I was in the country I think I would still call this department, even though there are departments everywhere else. It is because I know that I have had dealings here before, and know what to expect.''

Part of continuity was contained in records which the group recognized were an important part of social work, particularly when part of a child's life had to be spent away from his family. The importance of records lay not only in their usefulness for social workers but in their value to the individual child in care, to his knowledge of himself and his background and in the reality of his life as he was living it. A child may need to be told several times and in order to preserve the information needed and to do justice to the problems of any case, records were needed.

''Because I was adopted when I was a few weeks old, I often wondered about my real mother,'' said Margaret, ''and I think 'What did she look like? Why did she really have to give me up? Who was my father? Why didn't they marry?' I feel as though I have started three existences; one when I was first born, then one when I was adopted, and then one in care and it's very confusing to think that. In fact, I feel as though I have got three sets of parents.''

What sorts of records should be kept? Group members considered there should be ''a lot of information'' but of what kind?

Miranda expressed strong resentment of the practice in one children's Home of recording something about each child each day. It was ''not so much the record. It was what they put in it. I mean they didn't miss a trick, whether you nicked the apples from the kitchen garden or pinched a cake out of the larder and you were caught. Such stupid minor things like that.''

''I don't understand,'' said a member of the group who had been brought up in a foster home.

''I'll tell you,'' said Miranda. ''I only found this out when Annette was my housemother, so I must have been about thirteen or fourteen. Before then, I couldn't have cared less what they wrote about me. On her day off, her right-hand girl, which I was at the time, used to make a scrambled egg on toast and I took it up to her and she had some files on the table that I was to put the tray on. I moved these files and unfortunately mine happened to be on top, and so I said 'What's this?' and she sort of went red and didn't quite know how to explain and while I was shifting them I sort of pushed them down and there was someone else, another name that was also in the group so I just came to the conclusion that they were our records.''

Miranda admitted that she had made an opportunity to go back and read her own file.

''She (Annette) sent me up for something later in the day. She gave me her key and my file was still there. I thought perhaps she might have locked it away but she hadn't. I'm just trying to recollect what she wrote. I think it was something about me thumping one of the other kids which I thought was (hard). Obviously all children fight but to put this down on record! It must have been very boring reading for whoever had the files when they were completed.''

Margaret had had experience of working for children in care and explained to Miranda, ''You have to put the aggressive moments as well as the placid moments to get a true picture of that child, so therefore day-to-day accounts of what the actual child has done are very important.'' She also pointed out that ''You need to know the gap of time between the incidents to know whether its either getting better for the child or getting worse.''

The group members agreed that memory plays tricks and accurate records are important, but Miranda resented the fact that the child care officer or children's officer might see these notes and might say something like "'I hear you've been pinching things; I hope you're not going to be a thief when you grow up,' or 'You've been bullying the other children, you can't fight your way through everything, you know,' and just things like that." The power she believed the children's officer had made her fear that the reports might lead to her being removed from where she was and where she wanted to stay.

On the other hand some members felt that because of records the children's officer, though remote from them compared with their child care officers, would be able to understand about children's needs and problems, and this would enable the right things to be done for them.

Photographic records were also held to be important, not just photographs of events and groups, but of individual children at different stages of their lives, records which could be given to them to fill in the gaps which are normally filled by family memories and records. "I'd love to know what I was like when I was about eleven at school; I haven't got any photographs of that age," said one member.

"My first one is about six, I think," said another. "I'd like to know what I was like when I was a baby. Most families have one, in the cot, on the lawn or something. My brother (foster brother) has one and I feel a bit jealous about that."

"I suppose it would be too much trouble if every time someone came into care, take a quick photo of them," another suggested.

School photographs were prized because they were taken every year, though one member predictably said, "The only thing I didn't like about school photos was it was all posed. You had to have your hair brushed properly and your tie straight. You had to have your arm on the table pretending to read a picture book."

"It says a lot more than words sometimes to have a photo," concluded Derek.

Discussion showed how important it could be to

individuals to have information which opened up missing parts of their lives; how important it was in providing an aspect of continuity and a sense of their past as well as present identity. One member asked whether a "small file" couldn't be given to people who had been in care, containing significant information which they could keep. Amongst the information members thought important for the record were "temperament of parents; if the child has an outburst they (the current care giver) wouldn't misinterpret it"; "how things went in the past"; a basic outline "of childhood growth and development, medical history and parents' health record, including information about any family health problems which might be unknown to the child" but which it was important for doctors to have. Records represented part of the important knowledge which was needed to help compensate for the fragmentation of life which many child care problems produced. The group members felt they should not only be part of the professional practice of social workers, but that adequate provision should be made for them in the organization of the department.

Discussion of records and the information children in care needed to have led to consideration of how much children should or can be told at the time and who should tell them. The general feeling was that children should be told the facts as they went along.

"I think the truth hurts when you are older much more than if you are told the truth all the way along."

"Exactly, I think this, yes. I think throughout my life lots of things have hurt, not outwardly but perhaps inwardly, at not knowing things."

Who should be the person to tell children the facts about their circumstances, if it could not be their parents, was a question which brought clear opinions from group members. They thought that even though the child care officer should be in constant contact with a child, the task of telling the child facts which were hard to face and might be distressing should be carried out by someone with whom the child was living all the time.

"I think it ought to be the person that you're living with. It shouldn't be your child care officer who comes to visit you to tell you all about you. The person that's looking after you should know, shouldn't they? Its no good someone coming from the outside and saying to me all these facts about myself; then when they go, the person that I'm living with doesn't know it."

"If the people that you are living with have this information to hand, I think, when they tell you these things it's more convincing, and it's with more authority I think than perhaps someone that's casually seeing you."

They added that it was important that the person who told a child information which might be hard to face should be someone with whom the child had physical contact, implying both that this person might know the child better and also that the child might need physical comfort at such a time.

It was clear that the group members envisaged the responsibility for children in care as being a shared task, not only between field and residential social workers but between social workers and more senior staff, including the person ultimately responsible for the department as a whole. This seemed to them not only an advantage but a necessary safeguard for the children's interests.

"I think a child would feel more secure if he knows more than one person is interested in him," said Margaret, "more than one person that's going to make the decisions in anything that concerns him. You've a chance to talk it over and to see points for and against."

"I think where you get a bad case where the child care officer couldn't communicate, at least there is the added thought in the back of your mind that its going back to someone. Surely that someone is going to say 'well, you're not doing very well with her, are you? Do you think Mrs So-and-So, or Mr So-and-So might do better with her?' If it wasn't going back to someone that child care officer would just carry on and on and things would just deteriorate rather

than somebody saying, 'Well, you've reached the point of
no return, you've got to change, got to do something'.''

Sometimes there was a quite deliberate attempt to attract the
children's officer's attention: "Running away, I don't know
how many people have gone through this stage. I certainly
have," said Andrew. "It was only a matter of two or three
miles across the fields. It was hay-making time and they had
these heaps of hay in the middle of the fields and we all hid
inside this heap of hay knowing that everybody was out
searching for us. We were determined not to go back and we
were going to sleep the night under that pile of hay because
we wanted it to come to the notice of (the children's officer).
In our childish way we thought somebody's going to get to
hear about this, we'll have somebody down here to sort
things out. I can't even remember what the instance was that
I wanted sorting out now, but I remember this impression in
my mind, you know, that if we did something dreadful, like
running away, that this would get the attention we wanted. It
had been planned, something like a union meeting you
know.'' Another group member who had run away as an
adolescent provided a similar example:

"When I ran away I felt, well, somebody's got to do something if I run away, so I did and I think it was Auntie Mary
and Mr York who came and picked me up, and I thought the
children's officer's there, surely she will know about it and
perhaps she'll do something.''

They were interested too in the relationship between field
social workers and the children's officer, "the great white
goddess" or "the boss" as some of them called the role. They
saw this role as part of the continuity they thought so
important. Child care officers and residential staff knew a lot
about them but they moved frequently whereas the children's
officer had been the same person for as long as they could
remember. She was someone they did not see often, but "we
knew who you were. This was the point. We knew who was
back there, we didn't have to come to find out," said one
member.

"I haven't known you personally until these meetings, but I've known you've been there," said another.

"Like a grandparent," said a third.

"Two heads are better than one; I thought the children's officer was the boss and she was all powerful, but she didn't frighten me";

"I was frightened of her";

"I think I was as well really";

"I don't think I was afraid of you; I just resented that you were the person that had the say in where I was to go";

"I thought "Oh it must be the woman who supplies the money; she probably sees I'm all right or tells my child care officer off";

"I just felt choked that anyone was over me and that was it," said others.

At the same time, as the last member put it, in the final resort they saw the children's officer as someone they would go to, who, partly because of the records kept by the staff, partly because of the role she held would "know what to do and how to do it", although the child care officer was "probably just as capable, if not more capable because she knew me better." Asked why, if this were so, she took the view she had expressed of the children's officer, the group member replied that the children's officer had been there a long time unlike the child care officers, "I had so many, that was the trouble; I had three in the four years that I was in care."

Group members had sometimes felt frustrated when their child care officers had appeared unable to make a decision on the spot about something they felt was pressing, but they recognized that it was valuable for them to discuss the issues involved and consult. On the other hand they were critical of how this had been put to them as children. "They should have had greater understanding with the child not to say 'well, I've got to go back and consult', but say 'Let me think about it!'" One member also felt that "instead of going away and saying 'I'll see what we can do' they should admit they were worried. I always felt that you were my parents and that you were doing what my parents should do."

The importance, but also the difficulties, of personalizing a social service to children was an issue which arose many times and in various ways during the meetings of the group. There were major organizational problems like the need to try to retain some continuity in relationships between children and their social workers. There were also problems, as has been seen already, concerned with how personal such a relationship could be and what would assist its personalization. In the children's department in question there had been a long-standing practice of field social workers buying personal gifts for their children at Christmas and at birthdays instead of sending postal orders representing the sums of money allowed for these purposes. These gifts were personally chosen, purchased and sent with greetings cards from the social workers and the department. A number of social workers saw this practice as an opportunity to underline their personal interest in the children for whom they were responsible and took pleasure in it; some others saw it as a waste of time and an inappropriate way of carrying out a professional task. The group was invited to comment on how they had felt about these gifts when they were in care.

"I've still got them, I've always kept them";

"I've kept all the letters as well, all the letters I've been sent concerning my past life, I've got them in a great big envelope marked private';

"I think it needs something to come from here";

"You can see it's come from the department and as a child you are still under their wing and you can go to them if you have a problem; if you've got any problems even when you are out of care. It doesn't have to be anything expensive, just something trivial";

"I think you felt honoured with the gifts from the children's department."

The group listened with interest and understanding when a professional member asked if she might read an extract to them from a letter she had recently received. It was from a girl with whom she had been working who had just reached eighteen years of age and gone out of care after some years in the care of another local authority. She had been asked in the context of the group discussions what she thought about the issue of buying presents for children in care as an alternative to giving postal orders or some other less personal means of giving a present.

"You asked me what I thought of the idea that some child care officers suggested it might be better to give children in care money instead of a Christmas present. Obviously you can't generalize and the only helpful factor is the child's age. I don't know if you agree with me but on the whole I think if you give a ten-year-old child money he would spend it on sweets, get upset because he might drop it down a drain, or buy cigarettes to show all his school chums how clever he is, silly examples but in other words he is more likely to waste it. However I really do feel if presents were bought they would be serviceable in more than one way. There are many people whom I like and get along with but there are people I like and respect but find it difficult to communicate with and spend time trying to make them think I don't like them. You can give an impression that you couldn't care less. On my dressing table I have got gifts from these people and very often I can look at them and cherish them because they remind me of the person who bought them and I can show warmth to an ornament whereas I would go to extreme lengths to show the person I disliked them.

"I am sure there are children in care with the same outlook, even though they may only be five years old. I think they would be able to think like that, although for a five-year-old walking around in that frame of mind would be dreadful. In other words I think it is better buying a present that may be just another toy or worthless as a present, but a materialistic symbol of the person who has bought it."

One of the problems for field social workers, as group members saw it, was that by the nature of their role they were less likely to be used as a confidant by individual children than the staff of residential establishments or other people who ministered daily to children's needs; and they therefore needed to use methods which would personalize the realtionship as far as possible.

"The person who is in close contact where the child is living, be it a foster home, or be it a children's Home, that is the person that is going to get the questions isn't it? Especially at night time, or perhaps in the bath when there is personal contact with that child. You are either tucking it up, or you are doing little things that a mother normally does for a child, then the child is going to ask the questions, not when she, or he is going out, or sitting down with all the other children about. It is when you are on your own with the child and not when they have got other interests."

Miranda gave a concrete example, a member of staff called Norma. "She wasn't actually my housemother but she was a motherly type of person, she was big and cuddly she was, and I remember when she used to brush my hair, because I had very long hair then. I wouldn't let anyone but her do it because I used to scream my head off, and she used to sing to me to keep me quiet when she was getting all the knots and tangles out. I used to have some lovely conversations and I suppose it is just the way she actually talked to me."

Although they thought individual children were likely to find it easier to establish close relationships with residential staff and foster parents than with field social workers, the group members were anxious to discuss the role of field social workers with families and children, both in their own homes and elsewhere. They felt they could be a general support and friend to families in difficulties, particularly by helping them in practical ways, such as finding somewhere to live, finding means of coping with children during working hours and dealing with the many forms and papers on which benefits of various kinds depend.

"All I personally wanted when I was first left on my own was somewhere to live with Christopher," said Margaret. But later, "You need someone to explain if you don't know. If I hadn't known about nursery schools I wouldn't got Christopher in and I wouldn't have been able to go out to work. These are the things you need help in more than anything, the everyday basics to help you get back on your feet and start another life."

Another member said he believed people "are not aware of half of them (the services available) or what they are entitled to. This has been made plain by the fact that the Government are making different advertising approaches to make people aware."

There was also a need, the group thought, for "people who can talk to people in words of one syllable because they use a lot of these great long words and a lot of people don't know what they are talking about and then go away and say "I don't understand a word of what I was told, can you tell me what to do?"

"It's like these forms you get from the income tax people," said Valerie. "They are worded so that you just cannot understand them; you just have to sit and fathom each word out as it comes."

The very practical image of social work which the group thought important was also evident in their discussions of the roles of social worker and home-help combined. They saw major disadvantages in small communities in having home-helps recruited from the same locality. On the other hand they considered that very constructive help could be given in some family disasters if there was someone who would help to sort out domestic as well as financial and other kinds of chaos. They thought some of the experiments already carried out by local authorities in trying to keep families from breaking up by employing mobile home-helps with cars and caravans were the kind of scheme they envisaged. To be able to do this kind of work confidence would need to be established first between the family and the worker. Margaret and Valerie, both with the experience of being parents, felt that whether the work was being carried out in the family's own home, or in a residential setting as the group had earlier discussed, if the whole family and not just the children were involved, the social worker would need to tread delicately.

"The staff would have to put herself/himself last of all, not exert authority, not exactly disappear, but they would have to stand back and this would be terribly difficult to do unless you had acclimatized yourself to do it." To be able to do this it might be better to have started by getting involved with the family in its own home.

"Perhaps (the social worker) could help the mother if she explained her problems to her. It could take some tension off the mother and then perhaps leave more time for her children," suggested Valerie. Margaret replied:

"But you have to gain the confidence of the mother to get her to tell you her problems."

"Yes, but this is the idea of the case worker moving in," Valerie said.

"Would it not be better to have something like the home-help service where someone goes daily to old people?" asked Margaret.

"Should this be the same person or might it be two different people, for example?" asked the children's officer.

"No, I think it should be the same person because you can't get a relationship going with someone who has so many problems if so many people are popping in and out. It makes more problems. It needs to be one person that they can rely upon and then after they have gained their confidence then you can have a number of people popping in and out," Margaret concluded.

At one stage in the discussions it was suggested that the group might try to draw together what they thought were the characteristics of an ideal child care officer. It was significant that the first one mentioned was that it should be "someone who spoke to you on your own level. Sometimes child care officers spoke above you; I think it makes you feel better to know that somebody is talking to you in a way that you understand." This applied not only to the words people used but also to their manner. They needed to be able to convey that they were ordinary people, not too young to make an adolescent embarrassed at discussing personal problems, but able to be involved in juvenile interests and prepared to spend time with the children. It was necessary to know "they are not the ogres that you have a mental picture of" but "just as normal as everybody else." Miranda had appreciated "things that got me away from community living just for a few hours." Her child care officer, who was the same one that Anne could not relate to, took her out in a punt one day and fell in the river. "It was so funny to see her waist deep in mud and water, full of weeds, absolutely drenched from head to toe, and me rocking the boat from side to side because I was laughing so much; I didn't even think to help her out of the water."

Some of the women members of the group had had experience of being taken to their child care officer's home accommodation. They did not express a view about this but there was a general feeling of the need for social workers to share in the children's interests, be practical and be people whom the children could really get to know. Group members' feelings about the sex of social workers was fairly conservative and it was clear that they felt if they had had someone of the opposite sex it might have inhibited them from discussing intimate personal problems. On the other hand in the residential setting where there was a choice of adults, a mixed sex staff group added richness and interest to life.

After a lot of discussion Derek said realistically, "I don't think you will ever get an ideal welfare officer; all cases are different. They may make a break with one child and then move on to another case and there may be a block."

In general whilst members of the group saw the field social worker as a very significant person in their lives and had often wanted more rapport with him or her than they had, as well as more time and more interest, it was clear that their expectations did not include the warm, physical, day-to-day substitute parenting that they hoped for, and sometimes received, from residential social workers.

9 Education and Teachers

To go to school every day is a statutory requirement for all children, unless they are unable to do so by reason of illness or some other legitimate cause. This is a continuing reality for each child from five to sixteen, most of their childhood years. Thus five days a week, forty weeks of the year, a child is expected to arrive at school even if families move frequently, parents become ill, desert their children, lose the family home or job, change partners, go to prison, or put the child in care. Such expectations can be both a stabilizing influence and a demanding constraint. Children may be unsettled, filled with grief, overwhelmed with anxiety, deprived of normal family support; they may be attending one of a succession of schools in none of which they have been able to put down any roots, or the school may, by good chance, be one of the few long-term, familiar and reassuring elements in a background shattered by events beyond their control. Either way, to give their full concentration to their work or to be able to maximise the opportunities that are offered is likely to be difficult. Yet for most children the years of school are the only chance they have for laying the foundations of knowledge and pre-employment skills, and once gone cannot be recovered except by unusual determination and persistence in later life. It is a period of life when many children, even those whose lives are relatively carefree, need encouragement and support to focus their minds and energies consistently and fully enough to benefit adequately from education. There are many distractions and rewards may be infrequent and often hard to obtain. If there are conditions in schools which teachers find unsympathetic, large classes, insufficient equipment, unmotivated children, the children themselves are affected by these and perhaps the precious years of preparation for life may slip by, imperceptibly measured by day-to-day events, until suddenly they are almost over and the more demanding world of employment, or lack of it, and adult life, with its responsibilities as well as its privileges, is round the next corner.

Research over recent years has clearly demonstrated the importance of a child's home in supporting his capacity to benefit from education and to make the best use of his ability. It is no accident that so many children who have suffered disruption of their homes find themselves educationally disadvantaged in spite of attending school regularly. The disruption and their feelings about what is happening to them may also effectively mask their natural abilities, not only from their teachers and those responsible for their care, but also from themselves.

The members of the group had all been to day primary schools and most to what were then known as secondary modern schools. Alex had attended grammar schools and Miranda had been for a time to a secondary boarding school. Barry, Margaret and Carol had subsequently undertaken periods of further education. It will have become clear from previous chapters that as adults the group showed themselves to be people with perception and ability and some of them had deep feelings of regret about the educational opportunities they felt they had missed or not used as fully as they might have done. When they looked back to try to describe how it felt at the time they were able to identify some of the difficulties and problems which had made school a largely unsatisfactory experience for them.

They recognized very clearly that their attitude to school had been related to where they were living and whether the adults caring for them were concerned about their educational progress. On one occasion they had a long discussion which demonstrated this. Barry described how when he was in a children's Home he was fifth from the bottom in a class of over forty, but when he was boarded out his class results got better each term until he was third from the top. He could not explain why this had happened except that his foster mother and an older boy in the family had both taken an interest in his progress and encouraged him in a variety of ways, some direct, others indirect. Two other group members, both men, confirmed that when they were in residential Homes' groups they found it hard to become really interested in school. One of them, Andrew, described himself as "absolutely useless in everything at school" until to his own surprise he had developed an interest in woodwork and metalwork and had finished top of the class in one and quite high up in the other. But he "felt retarded" in other subjects because he hadn't been able to be interested. "I wasn't really committed in my own mind to what I wanted to do with myself."

The experience of being one of a group from a children's Home attending a local school had a number of adverse consequences. It has already been seen how it could lead to individuals being treated differently from children who were living in their own homes; excused homework, assumed to be unable to answer for decisions about themselves like involvement in school outings and separated out from other children when school medical examinations were being carried out. The adult reasoning which led to these differences was not understood at the time and even if it had been would probably have been rejected by the children concerned. It was resented as a form of discrimination, something which increased self-consciousness already painfully over-developed by the experience of having to leave home and be brought up in care. But there were other effects with perhaps more serious long-term consequences. Andrew analysed the group pressure as follows:

"The group reaction that was within oneself sort of came in to encourage you not to knuckle down to anything directly responsible and get on with things. I think in certain circumstances you'd have been more independent of the whole group and perhaps less aware of being separate from any other individuals if you'd come from a normal home; if I'd been with a foster parent, a solitary individual rather than say one of twenty, all boarding the same school bus, all fighting for the seats, all diving for the ashtrays at the back of the seats. We were smoking then. We couldn't buy cigarettes but as boys we were very apt to pick up any dog-ends that there were about. In the Home you got into a sort of gang and you had several outstanding members and they smoked, so, naturally one or two of the other people got smoking; it was the fashion of the group then. In all those sorts of things — citing smoking is one silly little example. This sort of thing carries right through into education you know. Even at school I think we gained some sort of comradeship about being a little group rather than being a mixture in a classroom, and say, for my argument's sake, you weren't getting on very well or something like this, in maths, you'd talk it over amongst yourselves, 'Well, we couldn't care less' and it was all sort of bravado, being a whole group as it were. You threw all your emotions into that one group rather than having some sort of independence or some mind of your own. And you took refuge in that. It encouraged you to neglect getting on.''

Another member who had experienced the same pressure said, "I didn't like school and I didn't bother to learn. I'd rather just mess around." He thought if he had been in a foster home he "would have settled down and studied more" but "because I was in the children's Home and the lads from the children's Home went to the same school and the same class, and we messed about at the children's Home as well, then you think school is another children's Home, whereas if I'd been fostered I wouldn't have had them (with me) and I'd have had to start off again. I regret it, you know. That part of my life I feel I made a mess of, terribly.''

Andrew's children were having a very different start in life from their father's. "My children are totally different to me.

My eldest starts grammar school after this summer term, but he's got notions regarding going to university and all this. Even the other one who's only nine, he's commenting in the direction that he wants to do something with his life, whereas, at that age, I wasn't at all interested in what I was going to do with myself."

Andrew remembered three schoolmasters who had given him some encouragement; in two of their subjects, woodwork and metalwork, he had made headway. The third was someone "that did a lot of radio and electronic work. He used to take groups of us boys out of the school and we used to cycle all round the countryside with radio transmitters and plot bearings and directions and all this sort of thing. I think looking back that I could have done so much better had I concentrated on education when it was offered. The opportunity was there (but) I don't think the environment encouraged us to take advantage (of it). We were all for a good time, I think, all the time, instead of getting down to something concrete. We were only interested in the boyish pranks that boys get up to, rather than anything constructive."

Even Alex, who had the opportunity to go to grammar schools, felt the effects of group pressures and the interactions of groups of children with the world around them. In the residential community in which he lived some children went out to grammar and some to secondary modern schools. There was rivalry between them but they united against the rest of the world. "We were a group, twelve or thirteen, sometimes less, sometimes more, and we were recognized mainly by the fact that we were much louder-mouthed than most of the others at school, and because we used to come on the school bus and create havoc in school generally. We tended to lean upon each other quite a bit for support." But in addition, "There was this terrible segregation and it affected us. We were great friends in the Community and we'd get on the bus, you know, and because I had a different uniform on and different tie, albeit scruffy, and the chap next to me was going to secondary modern school, there was immediately a gap between us, you know? There used to be some occasions when we'd have quite big fights about this and lots of hatred would grow up.''

At the same time the Community encouraged the children to feel a sense of pride in belonging to it and they would invite their contemporaries at day school to come and see where they lived because it was quite impressive.

Margaret, who had been born and adopted in another country, experienced not only the problems of going to school from a children's Home, but also those of having to adapt to a different educational system as well as numerous different schools. She had great regrets about her education.

''Education, that is something that I desperately, when I was in care, wanted somebody to help me with. And yet there didn't seem anybody that I could turn to. I came from Canada to England, the method of teaching was so different that it took me until the term before I left school to really get a grasp of what was going on, because of all the different schools I'd been to in this country as well. And that last term if there had been somebody, in fact I think I did say to someone, 'I don't want to leave school, I want to stay on.' And I really wanted somebody desperately then to say 'Come on, work hard at it and perhaps you can!' I remember that as a real grudge that I felt at the particular time. I didn't want to go out into the wide world, I wanted to stay at school, I wanted to better the educational opportunities that I felt there were. I would like to have been made to sit down at night and do homework. At school I found they made allowances for the fact that I was in care, and that I came from Canada, too many allowances. I felt that if only they had come down with a rod of iron it would probably have helped: 'You sit there until your homework's done,' or 'you sit there until that's done and if you can't work it out ask me how.'' I used to long to be like other children that I knew had to take homework home.'' Margaret wanted to ask for it but thought it was no use because she did not think there would be anyone at the children's Home to help her, and she would need help. Ironically two of the house parents on the staff of her Home were qualified teachers. Margaret summed up her feelings by saying, "I felt that I wanted somebody to expect a lot more and demand a lot more because I felt I had a lot more to give, and there was no one, well, not no one to give it to, but no direction in which to give it. I didn't know which way to turn."

Occasionally the "Homes children" scored: "a lot of us Home people knew religious instruction inside out. Any questions that were thrown at us religiously, immediately our hands would shoot up, we knew them all, and the housepoints you gained! I should think the Homes children were top of the class religiously," joked Andrew.

The members of the group who had gone to school from children's Homes tended to feel that their problems might have been less great if they had been in foster homes and attended school in ones and twos, not as members of a larger group of children. Those who had been adopted or fostered, however, had mixed experiences to contribute. Some of them had been caused pain by other children who had discovered that they were in substitute families; sometimes they were proud of having been "chosen" and because of that felt "different" in an acceptable way. Either way they also had their problems in relation to their school life.

Carol had been a restless and puzzled child in her adoptive home and was one of those to whom other children had been unkind because she was adopted. She recalled that she did not like school, "but towards the last half of my (last) school year I picked up quite considerably. Everyone was quite surprised I think. Looking back on it there were lots of things I wish I had done and settled down to and actually I miss most of the things that I had at school and can't do now. I used to hate hockey, yet I love it now. The same with gymnastics and things like this. The same with English, poetry and that, I used to find boring at school but now I wish I'd listened more and could understand it better. At school we used to go through Shakespeare and Keats and things like this. I enjoy reading these now and don't really understand as much as I probably would if I was reading it at school. But I just didn't give a damn when I was at school. I couldn't be bothered.'' She thought she didn't get on well at school because she didn't make friends very well, "didn't feel included in things that were going on. It sounds stupid because I know I was really. I know now but I didn't then!''

Martin, a happy foster child, nevertheless had not got on very well until his final year in the primary school. "The last year in the primary school there was one teacher in particular that really pushed me on in maths and various subjects, but apart from that there was nothing there.'' When he reached secondary education he was aware of the selection process which was taking place and allowed himself to be classified for a "low" class without the resentment that many children feel.

"Then, of course, I went up to the higher school; all there was then was the routine of getting to school. I was big enough then to do a bit of work at night, but I was out and gone. They never pressed work on us because they thought it was the low class to start with and it was the low class all the way up and that was it. They never pressed any work and I never asked for it. Somebody's got to do the light work in the world and somebody's got to do the hard work, that's the way I looked at it. Not all of us can be bright and do the light work!'' After one year in the secondary school he was put in the group specializing in agricultural interests "and that was where my mind was set then. I knew, well, it was as good as a message sort of thing, that that was where I was meant to be and that was what I set my mind on.''

He thought his foster parents had given him all the encouragement they could, "but I wasn't interested. I was a fool that way but that was one of those things. I was more interested in the land — to get out was the main object.'' Martin made it clear in group discussion that he regarded

Barry as being someone "with real brains".

Barry had gone on to further education but at school he remembered he was never good at maths and hated it, nor was he good at English. His view was: "The subjects that you are good in you like, obviously. I enjoyed history, geography and R.I. and I got on all right in cricket!" He felt that the area in which he went to school was one in which pressure was exerted on children to go on the land, and that they were not told enough about other opportunities to enable them to make appropriate choices about their careers. Barry was quite clear how he had felt. "I'd got brothers on the land and I thought 'Well, I'm not going there', you know. I didn't really know what to do. I didn't want to go on the land and I didn't want to be in an office. If my foster father had had his way I would have gone and worked in an office with him, but I fought against that." Barry was very glad that he had had the opportunity to go to a college of specialized further education where he learned to become a skilled craftsman.

Andrew, who was several years older than Barry and being cared for during the very early years of the children's department, felt himself "to be about three years retarded" when he left school at fifteen years old. He welcomed "recent government actions to extend the school leaving age to sixteen" because it was only by fourteen or fifteen onwards that "you begin to think you've got a responsibility in life and you've got to look at yourself and decide."

He had not had the same consideration given to his potentialities as Barry had and he deeply regretted his lack of opportunities. "Possibly the organization at that time didn't really cater for the attention that people are getting today," he said sadly. "Possibly the children that are in care today develop and advance much better than we did in our day and probably end up in better positions than we did and are better educationally."

The connection between achievement at school and subsequent employment prospects was one which members of the group saw as very significant. It was also a common experience for them to wake up and find school days had run out and everything was too late. Margaret and Andrew had both described how they felt.

Derek, who was in a foster home, not a children's Home, expressed his experience in this way: "They didn't really impress it on you how important education was until your last year at school. Then when you realized how close it was to leaving time you suddenly put on a spurt, but by then it was probably a bit too late to gather everything in. I think it's a good thing to start from a very early age how important school is and how it will affect you later on in life. I wish somebody had told me how important it was going to be after. I looked on it just as a routine, just a chore to go through every day. I got praise in good subjects and tickings off if I was down in a subject, but they never sort of started to teach me anything. I suppose they would have helped me if I'd asked but I didn't know how important schooling was so I never used to go looking for further education. The only homework I ever took home was forced on me, I never asked for any; I didn't because I knew I would only catch it on the bottom the next day! It wasn't through choice. If I'd realized how important it was going to be when I started work! I failed to get a couple of jobs because I wasn't up to it on maths or something, everything else was average, but if I'd realized when I was still at school it was going to let me down I'd have taken private lessons or something." Asked about the effect on him in school of being a foster child he said, "Being in a foster home you're not any different from any of your class mates. I think the teachers knew I was in a foster home but they didn't treat me any different; they didn't let up on me or anything. I was pretty proud of it, I felt different from the rest of the class. I remember walking out with my head held high for about a week, the fact that I'd been chosen."

Andrew reiterated that he wished he had had someone to impress on him how important education was and Margaret explained further what she meant by being "pushed" to do things. She said that when she was in care it was the children's officer she most "looked up to" and that, turning to the children's officer, was "because you were the only person who said, 'I would like you to do so and so.'" There never seemed to be anyone else that really said that. The child care officers said 'Well, what would you like to do?' and the (children's Home) staff would say this too. Now I've got children of my own, my little boy responds far more to 'Well, Christopher, I would like you to do something, please, for me, will you do it?' than if I say 'well what would you like to do?'; and this is just exactly how I felt when I was younger. My mother used to give too much leeway. She would say 'Oh, don't make her do so-and-so' to my father and I think this is why I respected him and looked up to him more than I did my mother because, well, she never pushed and I feel that children need somebody that will push them because that gets the best out of them. Not only children, but adults as well, need somebody."

The members of the group had had unhappy experiences with some teachers, who were insensitive and occasionally even unkind in their attitudes about the children's personal backgrounds. The kindness and understanding of other teachers, however, outweighed negative experiences in their memories and demonstrated that awareness of the needs of children in care and sympathetic responses to them can make school a very positive personal experience on occasions. Miranda, who rarely "let adults off" for their deficiencies, remembered a "very nice headmaster" at her junior school. "He used to come down to The Beeches to see the children when he wasn't working. I don't know what his purpose was, he used to just come and chat, take photographs and take us for walks, and he was the person I could talk to."

Derek had had an experience at school which had made a significant impact on his feelings about teachers. He normally tried to keep a very brave face to the world, but occasionally he was unable to. He described what happened. "The day after my foster father died I was sent to school anyway because (Mum) wanted me out of the way, and I was sort of miserable all day at school. I never used to talk to anybody, even to me mates, I used to keep quiet, they didn't know. Then one day the headmaster took our form (one of the teachers was away or something) and he was asking the whole class what their fathers did and jumping from one to the other. Finally he came to me and I just broke down and the whole class was looking at me and he went very red. He was very embarrassed; I hadn't told anybody, I had just gone along as I had normally done through the rest of the week. Then when we were all going out of the class he stopped me and said, "Wait until all the others have gone." Then he told me that if I ever had any problems to go and see him. He knew all about my past, I was surprised how much he did know. I never knew that he knew I was adopted (fostered), I was surprised. I felt completely different after knowing that I could go and talk to him. It was a sort of relief that he did know all about my past. He seemed very upset when I told him my father (foster father) had died. He said, "Why did you come to school?" I felt different after that, I felt easier for the rest of the day. The following week he caned me but I knew I could go to him if I had any problems in the future. I think they know more than they let on, teachers!"

Margaret's experience of teachers when she was faced with a similar loss, was not so positive. "When I went back to school after my father had died, he died on the Sunday and I went to school on the Monday, I was very upset. I got sent home from school because of it because I just kept bursting into tears all day, nobody knew why."

Finally Anne, who with her brother, had had the experience of going abroad with foster parents and being supervised by an organization which did not employ social workers, explained that when "us kids didn't have anybody to turn to" she turned to her teachers instead. "I remember once I had a very good school and I got on very well with the teachers there. It was a sort of comprehensive school as you would call it now but we used to call it Secondary Bilateral. I was there about a year and a half, and tension had built up inside me so much that I just had to talk to somebody and some perfectly trivial thing at school happened in a domestic science class, I can't remember what it was, and I started crying a bit, weeping, and the teacher was ever so sympathetic. She asked me to tell her all about it and when my tears had dried up a bit I went out and went home. It was the last period of school so I was OK. She must have spoken to the headmaster about it because soon after that a lot of the teachers assessed my work and I got a lot of individual attention from then, not to do with my own private affairs, but it made me feel as though, at last, I belonged to somebody or something or a group of society. I wasn't so cut off any more. I was very grateful to those teachers, especially the headmaster. He arranged that I could take 'O' levels and if it hadn't been for him I don't think I'd have had the courage to go into anything. I think I'd have been a very backward sort of person if it hadn't been for his egging me on to make something of myself, for myself. If my foster parents weren't interested I wasn't to worry. If nobody else was interested it didn't matter. He was interested, and I had to be for my own sake, for earning power and this sort of thing. It was really like a pep talk I got and he did quite a lot for me. I took some exams and passed them and it boosted my morale tremendously. I really felt as if I had something then, when I came back to England; but I felt as though I had lost something as well, I'd lost youth, you know what I mean?''

10 Some General Thoughts

Much of what the group discussed when they met concerned specific areas of their experience and these have been brought together in the previous chapters. In addition, however, some matters of a more general nature were raised, particularly in the last few meetings. Some of these touched on organizational and policy issues in social services, some on the general problems of children and young people who need substitute care, some related to the whole business of growing up, facing crises and meeting basic emotional needs. Like many other people, members of the group had little knowledge of how public organizations work, but they were interested in and curious about how local authorities discharged their child care responsibilities. They also realized that organizations can achieve their objectives in a variety of ways, some of which may influence the nature and quality of the service given at the receiving end. Sometimes, without knowing it, they identified some of the more intractable problems encountered in providing services, though they appreciated that problem solving can be very difficult. On one occasion they expressed what hard work they themselves found it, trying to think out the many issues which would have to be resolved to achieve a service development they considered desirable. Nevertheless as former clients of a public service their perceptions of how recipients of services felt, or would feel, were often different from some of the assumptions made in official policy and in the work of implementing it. Their experience had also shown that the way a service is actually provided on a day-to-day basis may be very different from policy statements which are intended to set the pattern of service delivery. This chapter draws together some general points and concludes the presentation of what the group discussed during their eleven meetings.

How much services cost, who provided the money to pay for them and how it was distributed were questions which had puzzled group members. The first question on this subject came from Miranda who wanted to know how summer holidays for children in care were financed. At the time the group was meeting one local authority children's committee had attracted national publicity by discontinuing provision of such holidays as a means of economizing on expenditure. Miranda was quite clear that as far as she was concerned she would "rather go without a new dressing gown or slippers or something rather than miss a holiday." She remembered with pleasure the group holidays from The Beeches when children and staff had lived in small groups and enjoyed being together at the seaside. They had been able to live and talk much more freely than usual and she valued this as much as the change of scene. Some members of the group who had been in foster homes at holiday time had fared differently, having a holiday away or staying at home and having days out according to the foster family's choice. Shortly before the group meetings had begun the local authority concerned had consulted foster parents' views about special allowances, holiday expenses and general boarding-out payments. The intention was to set up a foster parents' working party to discuss a wide range of issues, including money for the maintenance of foster children. The group thought this a good idea and Derek expressed the view that it was "a pretty important thing to have a foster parents' briefing every now and again." In the more specific discussions about foster parents and boarding out it had been suggested that foster parents should be represented on local authority committees rather than "people with no experience at all with the general costs of bringing up children."

The system of subsidizing young wage earners who were still in care had also puzzled some group members and they were interested to have an explanation of how this was done, and how the general unit costs of maintaining children in care, whether in children's Homes, or elsewhere, were constructed. As a background to this an explanation was given of the way in which money was first allocated through the national grant system and local rates levy, then delegated through individual committees to spending departments and eventually through the chain of accountability to be spent on individuals for whom care had to be provided. The relationship between resources and needs was seen by group members to be an integral part of the day-to-day life of a child in care, a practical example of which was their questions whether foster parents' motivation would be affected adversely by not receiving allowances and whether allowances should be continued after children were adopted.

The care provided for members of the group was financed by statutory funds, but some of them had also been recipients of charitable gifts. The Beeches children's Home had had a close link with a local firm for many years. Miranda described what this link had meant to the children when she lived there. "About a month before Christmas, Auntie would come in and say, "Right, here are pen and paper. I want you to write some nice letters to your friends at Browns and tell them what you would like for Christmas — and don't anyone ask for anything like a wireless set!" A typical letter ran something like,

"Dear friends at Browns,
    How are you! I am well. For Christmas I would like ——
———————— Thank you very much."

A sceptical group member asked, "Were the letters sent, or were they just screwed up?"

"Oh, yes, they were sent," said Miranda. "If you asked for a wrist watch, Christmas Day, over they would come, usually in the evening, I think. We had a sort of party in one of the rooms and Father Christmas comes along and hands you your wrist watch, or whatever ..."

The same children's Home was provided with parties by members of the American forces based in England. Miranda remembered them with warmth and gratitude. "They were so good, the Americans, even on your birthday. They usually came on a Saturday, so if your birthday was the next day you knew they would have brought you a cake. You would see this great big swanky American car come down the drive and they would come out with a great big cake. The cakes they made were fantastic, and they used to bring big presents, things you don't get in England."

"This was to ease their conscience as well, I suppose," said the group's sceptic.

"But they seemed genuinely interested in us," Miranda replied. "We would go to the base and we would tag on to some poor chap and we would just ask him questions all day and the poor bloke was obliged to answer!"

Derek asked whether the local authority children's Homes had fetes like some of the voluntary organizations. The children's officer had not encouraged money-raising activities of this kind feeling that they might reinforce some of the less happy feelings that children had about their status of being in care. There had, however, been some developments of groups of "Friends" of particular Homes which were leading to events like fetes and one or two group members had been involved. Margaret had been to the Cedars to a fete and afterwards to a showing of photographs. "I sat in when they were showing the slides for the first time on the carnival they had and the children were thrilled to bits. They were saying, 'Oh, look! That's me!' or, 'Look, that's so-and-so! Oh, look what he's doing!' and they were really excited." Another Home had allowed its grounds to be used for a village fete, the purpose of which was to benefit the village as a whole, not the Home. On this occasion it was said that the children had been pleased because it was their house and garden that were being used.

Discussion of how far children in Homes could become

more integrated into the community, through church or guides or scouts or school, or just by being in its midst, led to some further discussion of the changes likely to take place as the result of the Children & Young Persons Act, 1969. It had been explained that some community Homes (as they were to be called), especially perhaps those with education on the premises, might have facilities which members of the surrounding community might come in and use, or share from time to time, with the children and staff. The group was interested in this concept and thought that the Homes might feel less isolated in these circumstances, but they were quick to point out that it would be necessary for the children to be happy about the arrangements and not feel that they were being singled out because they were in care. Their own experiences had taught them that people often assumed that children were in care because they had "done something wrong" and wondered if the removal of distinctions between young offenders and those in care for other reasons might reinforce rather than diminish this tendency. On the other hand they saw no value in putting children in approved schools (under whatever name) although they had not personally experienced them.

"I haven't had anything to do with them, but I feel that if I was put there, I'd think, 'Right, I've been put here, I've got to make out I'm as bad as they've expected," said one.

"They are in the wrong company if they go in there too. They've got to keep their faces up as well and watch the others," said another.

They continued to be very concerned about the stigma of need, and thinking about children having to be received into care from their current standpoint as adults and parents they felt they would "like to see, from the parents' point of view, the stigma removed from Homes. The fact that you have got to send your child to a Home, perhaps through domestic problems or something, and the feeling that (people would say) 'Oh he's sent them to a Home, poor things', from a parent's point of view I think they must feel some sort of sense of guilt or shame at having to send their children into care, I should like to see that removed," said Andrew. "If I had to take that step it would break my heart and it must feel the same to them as it does to me."

"And I should also like to think that by sending my children to a Home they are receiving a lot better treatment or facilities than a lot of normal homes are getting. I don't mean to go to the extremes where they are living a life of luxury and it is costing the government a fortune. But I would like to see them go, not into a big communal building where you become non-existent, I would like to see my children in a smaller community, or if it was in a large community, then one which was segmented into small communities. Then the individual attention that parents could, and should, give in a small normal family, the authorities are able to give, and it is more natural for the child." Margaret regretted that the general public was still so ill-informed about children in care and the services provided for them. "I hear parents say, 'You will go into a children's Home if you don't behave'," she said, "and children grow up with the idea that children are in Homes because they are naughty, because their parents are bad, or they got into trouble in some way and so each generation thinks that a children's Home is nasty." There was anger in Andrew's comment: "It makes you wonder whether you are living in the seventies. It makes you feel that you are living in 'Pickwick Papers' time.' "Big bad ogres with sticks and slippers to wallop you!" responded Margaret.

Some members, while not disagreeing with Andrew's points about children's Homes, favoured foster home care because they thought it more likely that a child would receive individual attention. But whatever method of substitute care was provided they wanted time and effort to be spent arranging for children to visit where they were going before they had to go there, not only to have an opportunity to see the place and meet the people, but to be able to become accustomed to the idea, to feel that their parents knew where they were going, how far away it was and to satisfy many other natural questions that anyone would want to ask in the circumstances.

In this context the group gave some thought to how far people who had been in care themselves might help children who were currently in care. They felt they would be better able to understand what the children were experiencing and perhaps be able to help interpret how they were reacting. Derek wondered if they might be used sometimes as escorts when children were moving from one place to another. They could perhaps be someone the child could talk to "off the record" about how he was feeling and what was happening. In fact, though no longer a child, Anne had, as a result of meeting Margaret in the group, been able to get great comfort by talking over with her the predicament she was in, knowing that she would understand and that no one else would be involved.

Group members recognized that being able to help others would do something for them as well as for those they wanted to help. Margaret, who had described how she had become an advice-giver in the community in which she lived, said, "I enjoy doing this because it helps me more than anyone will ever realize." They all agreed, however, that whether it was a person who had been in care or other members of the community, anyone who offered to take an interest in a child in care should regard the undertaking as very serious and not start on it unless there was not only the intention but also the capability of continuing with it. They considered it damaging to say to a child in effect, "I will try to come next week but don't bank on it." One member was very honest and said, "I'm not very reliable really. I do things on impulse."

The members of the group always showed concern about how to prevent families having to put their children into public care as well as concern for the children when they were in care. They had expressed the view that many people were unaware of services and benefits which could help them and to which they might be entitled, and were critical of the language in which some official information and forms were written. Margaret, in this context, suggested that apart from the offices of various services there were the Citizens Advice Bureaux to which people could go for help. Valerie, however, thought these of limited use because they were only open "perhaps two afternoons a week. It is at night time and weekends when you get left on your own and you don't know where to turn!" Asked to whom they would turn at such times, the group expressed confidence, from their own experience and that of people they knew, that the police would help them get in touch with whatever service they needed "because they have the telephone numbers".

One-parent families, in Barry's opinion, had a special need for help of various kinds, particularly, he suggested, for holidays and clothing for their children. He was also concerned that the living accommodation they were able to find was not always conveniently situated for the purposes of employment, and then the difficulties and expense of travelling, apart from other problems of bringing up children alone, could make work very difficult to obtain. He and other group members thought the problems of loneliness and isolation were of major importance to these families. Margaret knew from her current experience how true this was.

"I think the biggest thing for a mother on her own with children is to be made to feel she can cope, and that she is capable of doing this," she said, "because it is so easy to give in. There are times when you are cross with the child just because you feel tired and exhausted. You shouldn't really be cross because they haven't really done anything wrong. It is just because it has got on your nerves. If there is somebody else there — Tom used to say when Christopher was tiny, "For goodness sake sit down and I'll make you a pot of tea. He will be all right in a minute. Just don't worry about him," and things like this. But when you have got to cope with it alone, it is so easy to become unbalanced about it."

Helping families to manage when they were in difficulties had led to discussion of domiciliary services when the group was talking about field social work, but the provision of domiciliary services was not seen as a simple issue. Families needed help and it was better in principle to help them in their own homes. Yet the very intimacy of some of their problems, the extent of their need, were likely in the group's view to make it difficult for some families to accept domiciliary services if local people were employed to provide them. They saw a serious risk of gossip and argued that privacy and confidentiality could be undermined by some of the methods used to provide services, like recruiting home-helps from the same community as the families receiving them.

Their sensitivity to the problems of people who might be different from the majority also led them to think about the problems of coloured children.

"You get some small black child who goes into a Home somewhere, if you had a coloured welfare officer to guide him through he might feel more at ease than with a white one," said Derek. He was aware of the possible political issues involved and wondered if it would be against race relations legislation to advertise specifically for coloured social workers whom he thought might not otherwise very readily apply to become social workers because they might be afraid they would not be accepted.

The group did not pursue the question of recruitment of social workers, but national publicity given to various cases during the time they were meeting had led them to discuss some of the issues highlighted by the cases. One was the recruitment of adopters, and the standards applied by local authorities and adoption societies in selection. Derek had been relieved to know that adoption societies had to be registered, but he also wondered how strict their vetting procedures were and whether sometimes they were too strict. He asked whether single people could adopt and whether bachelors were allowed to adopt girls. Inevitably there was also discussion about whether teenage mothers who were unmarried could, or should, bring up their own children, and how much adopted children should be told, or be able to find out, about their origins. These issues were explored in a general way without firm views being expressed.

It was understandable that the group should have an underlying preoccupation with the needs of children who were in care and identifying the most important of these needs. They knew from their own experience how easily a sense of personal identity can be damaged, how cut off from love and the sense of value that goes with it a child can feel, how hopeless and confusing the future can seem and the sense of powerlessness which can be produced by other people's apparently arbitrary decisions. They expressed these concerns in a variety of ways but the messages were constant. Looking back on the people who had meant something to them while they were in residential care they discussed the possibility of bringing domestic staff much more deliberately into the task of providing children with relationships and also in seeking knowledge from them about individual children's progress while in care. They could see that it might seem unreasonable to expect someone who was primarily employed to carry out a routine domestic task to interest herself in a particular child. On the other hand, should not any opportunity be taken to help the child to make supportive relationships with adults, particularly since the locally based domestic staff might often stay longer in the child's environment than other staff who moved on more quickly? At the least they "could give an insight into a child's feelings" if their experience of him was taken into account as well as that of the professional staff. The same concern led group members repeatedly to emphasize the need children in care have for individual attention, and therefore enough staff to be able to give it. They were anxious to make the point that this did not only apply to tiny children and those in the middle age range, but also to adolescents. Derek felt that "you are not really ready, even at fifteen when you leave school, to have the onus put on you or the responsibility of a decision (that is, about employment). You're so used to other people organizing your life that even at fifteen, seventeen, eighteen you need somebody else to help you make the decisions, to push you a bit." The members of the group tended to use the word "push" in contexts which suggested they felt children in care needed very strong support and backing, to help them overcome the uncertainty and indecisiveness which resulted from the traumatic experiences they had suffered. "Pushing" meant caring enough about them to help them make something of themselves. They could not rely on the natural supports and cushioning that other children and young people had in their own homes, and this became particularly clear in adolescence. They saw the years between leaving school and the mid-twenties as "the hardest part of one's life, when you are just finding your feet and beginning to realize what the big outside world is all about." The need for what so many people are able to take for granted was expressed by Andrew and Margaret on two different occasions, but with the same feeling of what they had missed. Andrew had been describing his feelings about the cook who had taken a personal interest in him; he said, "Possibly every child in our position craves for some sort of affection, and even that, from a child's point of view, was some sort of affection, was an indication of a mother's sort of affection." Margaret had been telling the group about the love she had for her adopted father: "He was the only solid thing that I had got. My mother was suicidal and she was always floating backwards and forwards to mental hospital. What I got from my father was security — this is what I personally felt that I would like from both my parents, security more than anything, security and the feeling that they were really both stable sort of people."

Margaret's father had died and she had grieved deeply. Some members of the group did not know whether their parents were alive or dead; some had no conscious memories of them. These were parts of themselves that were missing and could not be replaced. One discussion they had suggested that some losses are more easily accepted if a child can share in the experience with adults. Margaret said she remembered "that when my father died I wasn't allowed to go and see him. It took me years to believe that he was really dead. If I saw someone who resembled him I would think, "I wonder where he is, I wonder why he hasn't come back." By contrast, when a much-loved member of the staff died at The Beeches, Miranda and the children were involved. "We all came home from school, and her door was directly in front of you when you came in, and there was some string tied to the doorknob so that we couldn't open the door. We couldn't find any of the housemothers, so we all went up and changed and then went down to tea. Then they all came in looking very solemn. We knew something had happened but we thought perhaps she had been taken to hospital because she had been ill. Then they told us that she had died, and my natural reaction was to cry, and even the big tough boys cried, and that was something we all shared." Later on the children went to the funeral and participated with the adults in the loss of someone who had shared in all their lives for years.

Experiences shared are also a way of reinforcing a sense of identity. So are the memory of things past, places known and personal possessions. Barry, Derek and Margaret in different ways clung to the identification they had made with the group of children's Homes in which they had spent part of their childhood. None of them had entirely happy memories of them, though some times had been good, but nevertheless they all regarded them as part of their lives. Derek had taken away a piece of the wall and kept it; Barry recalled that "when the big playing fields we had there were sold and houses began to be built on them, it upset me." Margaret, who liked the Homes least of all perhaps, agreed, "Believe it or not when I go past there and I've got any strange person with me I've great pride in pointing out that that's where I used to live." Similarly the importance of gifts sent to members of the group by the staff of the children's department did not lie so much in what the gift was as in the fact that it was a symbol of having been treated as people who were important to the senders of the gifts. Derek had been able to "boast in front of other kids that you have got something they haven't;" Margaret described it as "a sense of identity with the person" who sent the gift. As a child in care "you must have something that is your own, that doesn't belong to everybody else."

A sense of identity and of value is supported by being loved, by having tokens of being valued, by being "pushed" into achieving something which otherwise would not have been achieved. Margaret had said that in her view "children need something that will push them because that gets the best out of them." The others had expressed similar views. Margaret expanded the idea in one of the later meetings of the group. "Unless you've got a sense of achievement everything seems to fall flat. You've got to have a goal to aim for and I found I lacked this when I was a child. I never felt that when I was in care I ever managed to achieve anything. I seemed to go around making so many blunders that everyone used to say, 'Well, let's sort it out,' instead of saying 'Well, you'll do something my way.' I was one of those sort of children that wanted to be led." She combined a statement of her desire to be helped to achieve with a description of what must have been the confusion she felt. "I got my own way with my mother. I can remember on one occasion I wanted desperately to go to the theatre in Boxhampton; we were living in Sunnington at the time. It was with the school and my mother said 'No, it's not the sort of play that a young girl can go to on her own.' So I just stood there and I got really bad tempered and in the end she relented and let me go. If she had had a logical reason for doing it I would never have got like it, but everything seemed to be illogical. And this is how I felt about being in care; to a certain degree things seemed to be illogical. There was just no reason for so many things that happened."

Some of the uncertainties and illogicalities of life which members of the group had experienced had perhaps made them particularly aware of themselves and their own feelings.

Anne had a natural sense of responsibility for her younger brother, but because she was tall for her age she believed people expected more of her than was reasonable. She also, because of the difficulties she had to face, had told the group she felt out of touch with her contemporaries. "I felt remote from anybody my own age group, as though I had passed that stage, felt more advanced than they were." She felt it had made her more independent, but although "it might broaden one's outlook in some ways, I think it definitely stunts it in others. You feel as though you've always been grown up; on the other hand I feel as though I'm never going to grow up," she said.

Alex, who was not as tall as Anne, assured her that being small did not necessarily mean life was simple either. "I can tell you being 5 feet 6 inches, small people try to prove themselves a lot." He also responded to her points about growing up. "What is childhood anyway? Childhood, I think, is something a person is ... he somehow feels he is free to express himself as he wants. He hasn't got responsibilities basically. When you get responsibilities you feel you are guiding someone else, so you can't express everything you want because you believe perhaps it's detrimental to that person, which I believe is the loss of youth. It's a sad thing and I think one has to retain a bit of it and try and sort out what are the useful parts which one wants to keep."

The group felt that when "you get responsibilities" and "are guiding someone else" you need to be able to empathise with them if the understanding they need is to be given. They had discussed this in the context of residential and field work staff and who was most likely to be able to encourage a child to confide in them, ask questions, unburden his problems and be able to be told the truth about what was happening to him. "Close contact" was important. They meant frequent contact, and it must be someone who was able to get to know the child well enough, and see him often enough, to respond when the child was ready to ask questions, and to receive answers. To do this that person needs to be able "more or less to anticipate a lot of things the child is going to ask.'' To achieve this means that the adults must have enough time, not as things are when ''the numbers are so vast, three children to one adult.'' As a child ''you've got to have somebody to talk to, to confide in.'' Some children have to bottle up what they want to say because they cannot talk to the people with whom they live. Although some unmarried residential staff had been much loved by group members, Valerie and Margaret both felt married staff with children of their own were more likely to be able to talk to children than unmarried staff. Margaret, who had worked with children in day nurseries and nursery schools, had found ''that the unmarried staff tend to always want to know better than the actual mother, unless they've got a very, very deep understanding. There are a few unmarried ones that I have come across that really have a deep understanding, but in general I felt they haven't even in children's Homes as well.'' Valerie went further and said she thought married staff were essential, ''I don't think they should be allowed to work with children until they have really got an insight into them.''

How would they get this insight, asked the children's officer. ''The only way you can get an insight into other people's feelings is to be emotionally involved in something yourself,'' said Margaret. ''I am quite convinced of this. Once you have any sort of emotional contact with another person, be it a child, be it an adult, you then start to find you have feelings towards other people and that you can understand better. I have found this with lots of sick people that I have come across. Once somebody opens out to you and you get emotionally involved and you don't know quite what to do about their situation, you don't know how to help them, then you stop and think about yourself and how you feel about people and whether you are really capable of listening to somebody's problems and helping them. Once you find you can do this, well, at least, I found this; once I had done this, I have been able to sit and talk to people on my own with them and try and help them.'' Alex put it this way: ''I sometimes find myself pulling up short and saying, "How would I feel if I was in his place?" You tend to brush things off quickly without giving them much thought. It is only when you really think "how would I feel?" I find it changes my whole attitude."

It was clear from their discussions and the way they listened to each other that members of the group found it helpful to have the opportunity to share their experiences with each other. For some it was the first time they had been able to talk over their feelings and memories with people who understood. One said, "It is helping me to understand how I felt when I was in care. You don't really talk about it to people outside because people just aren't prepared to sit and listen. They say, 'Children's Homes?', you know, 'How do you feel about that?' but they're not really interested." Another said the only reason he came at first was because the children's department had kept in touch with him after he reached eighteen years of age and he had found this helpful and felt "obligated to come. But," he went on, "it was only the first time I felt obligated. The rest of the time I came because I wanted to." This member, like the others, welcomed the chance to talk about what it was like to be in care, and said it was helping to give him "peace of mind". As a group, they believed it would be helpful to set up similar groups in other parts of the country, so that people like themselves could have a similar experience.

Epilogue

The group met for the last time in December 1970. A few months later the children's department which had provided for their care ceased to have an independent existence and became part of a social services department in the national reorganization of personal social services following the Seebohm Report. It was a time of change and upheaval in which many staff moved from the areas in which they had been working to different places and posts of different levels and responsibilities. Field social workers who had formerly worked with individual groups of clients, faced the challenge of all ages, groups and problems; middle management and support staff had to relate to day-to-day services for children, old people, the physically and mentally handicapped and the mentally ill. Bigger departments needed new management structures, more staff had to be recruited to deal with an increase of public demand for more easily identifiable services and new relationships had to be established, not only within social services departments, but between them and many other services and public bodies. This degree of change inevitably created uncertainty and anxiety as well as stimulus and excitement and, at least temporarily, fragmented and dispersed former expertise and familiar working arrangements. Many people were preoccupied not only with responding to changes in their work but also with uncertainty about their own roles and futures.

Hardly had the dust begun to settle than further major changes took place as a consequence of the 1974 reorganization of local government outside of London and of the National Health Service, with which all local authorities were required to become more closely involved.[1] Once more many individuals found themselves in new roles or were looking for different posts elsewhere. Boundaries were redrawn and some local authorities ceased to have an independent existence. Politicians, as well as paid staff, were involved in the general reshuffle. At the same time, whilst organizational changes were taking place, new legislation[2] had increased the responsibilities of social services departments which were having to work out the full implications for staff, resources and public accountability.

In these circumstances detailed issues of specialisms in social work and individual problems tended to be overshadowed by debate about wide concerns of management and resources. Some established good practice was lost and continuity was hard to maintain. A number of newly recruited, inevitably often untrained and inexperienced staff, were unaware of much that had gone before and had to improvise in the face of their complex task. Patterns of social work training which had begun earlier became more widespread and large areas of study concerned with one client group as a specialism became only a small part of tightly packed, more generically based courses from which trainees emerged, not as hospital social workers, psychiatric social workers or child care officers but as basic grade social workers expected to deal with a much greater range of problems and people than their predecessors.

In this context there was inevitably less concern than formerly to see children as having different needs from adults and as requiring special knowledge and skill to meet those needs. In addition the pressure of events and the lack of opportunity to work in depth led to greater emphasis by social workers on crisis and short-term work with a consequent reduction of emphasis on the needs of children in long-term care. The mobility of social workers had increased and they had less time to get to know children in care in general or individual children in particular. Inexperience in relation to courts and the range of facilities available for children and lack of knowledge of human growth and development and other facets of child care appeared to influence the outcome of many cases. Demand for secure accommodation began to grow, numbers of children and young persons in prisons and borstals rapidly increased and expectations of what could be achieved in working with "deprived children" appeared to fall while court committals to the penal system rose. These latter boys and girls were at the upper end of the age range in care; at the lower end increasing preoccupation with the problems of "non-accidentally injured" children ("battered babies") was reinforced by massive publicity and multiple public or other types of inquiries. Social services began to get a bad press on the one hand combined with unrealistic expectations by the public on the other and the social workers learned to feel very vulnerable in the face of the critical and sometimes sensational media.

Nevertheless the positive effects of change and fresh perspectives could also be seen in the development of new initiatives and modification of some longstanding problems. Intermediate treatment, for example, began to underline the need for improved facilities to help children and young persons to remain in their own homes and to reduce the flow of minor offenders into residential care. Experiments with specialized fostering and a growing recognition of the importance of treating foster parents as partners, sometimes quasi-professionals, indicated growth points in providing substitute parenting. The Children Act, 1975, introduced greater flexibility into the system of long-term care and opened a door to the exercise of children's rights in the determination of their own destinies. This trend was further pursued by the work of the National Children's Bureau in the formation of the "Who Cares" groups and the publication of their Charter of Rights.[3] Involvement of children and young people, on supervision orders with intermediate treatment conditions and in local authority care, as consumers was also a feature of projects carried out by the Social Work Service (Department of Health and Social Security) Development Group.[4] The old system of approved schools, which had been separate from mainstream child care services, was brought into the overall social services network and the unification under one umbrella of facilities like day nurseries, child minding, day care and hospital social work provided opportunities for more creative and constructive methods and use of resources. These and many other examples of new ideas and constructive developments provided indications of the creative possibilities of the new legislation and the reorganization of personal social services.

A major problem in providing personal social services is, however, the disparity between relatively unchanging human needs and the exigencies of human organizations. The context in which social services for children now operate has been modified not only by organizational change but by major changes in society as a whole, economic, cultural and structural. In the wider national scene important long-term and far-reaching developments, many of them outside national boundaries, continue to influence decisions concerning policy and resources, and changes in cultural patterns affecting the roles of men and women and the family in society have been speeded up since World War II. More specifically, developments in relationships between groups within society have brought new problems and challenged previously long-established attitudes.

Groups of professional people, including doctors, nurses, teachers and social workers, have broken with tradition and used or joined in activities like industrial action to further their claims for improvements in remuneration and working conditions. Unsocial hours, continuity of client/worker contact, acceptance of policy decisions made at government level have all been challenged and become part of a debate about what is reasonable to expect of individuals at work, even when the nature of the task they perform includes the client's basic dependency on them for certain forms of care and protection and fulfilment of primary human needs. Patterns of service provision are inevitably affected by such challenges, and many contributions made by groups and individuals, which were taken for granted a few years ago, are now in question and have to be re-assessed and reorganized taking new attitudes and assumptions into account. Ultimately it is possible that under the pressure of events new ways of meeting need may be found which may provide reasonable and acceptable services on models relying more closely on natural, that is, personal and community, resources and less on bureaucratically managed organizations. Some of the conflicting issues which would need to be resolved before this could happen, however, would include the mutual dependence and responsibility implicit in an industrial and technological social structure, the higher incidence of risk to family solidarity brought about by greatly increased divorce rates and changes in male/female roles, and the post-war increase in public demand for services to be provided by government rather than through individual initiative. Meanwhile each year a large number of children depend on bureaucratically organized services for public parenting while they are deprived of their own parents for long periods. The increasing number of incomplete families, in which either father or mother is missing, is likely to increase these numbers since the evidence demonstrates the vulnerability of children from these families compared with those from complete families. Recent statistics also show that high numbers of children on care orders remain in care for long periods, that is, more than twelve months.[5] On March 31st 1977 there were 36,300 on care orders who had been in care for over a year and a further 3,100 on other court orders. The total numbers on court orders showed an increase of 20 per cent since 1972, a steady and increasing rise each year. A further increasing group of long-stay children in care were those for whom local authorities had assumed parental rights under Section 2 of the Children Act 1948. These numbered 16,300 on 31 March, 1977, nearly 2,000 more than at the same time the previous year. Examination of these groups of cases would be likely to show that they are the ones with complex reasons for the children being in care, the ones which are likely to be more difficult to resolve, more difficult to restore to their families, and more likely to have to depend for most of their needs, not only physical, but emotional, social and educational, on the local authorities responsible for them. Experience and some available evidence show that those in care for three years or more are particularly likely to be continue in care for much longer periods. It is therefore important to know what they need and how best to provide it.

It has been said at the outset that this book makes no claim to generalize, but it may be legitimate to look briefly at how the group of ten people saw their own and other children's needs in comparison with how the needs of children generally are seen by those responsible for the relevant public services. In 1972 the Secretary of State for Social Services, Sir Keith Joseph, began to speak publicly about a concept he called "the cycle of deprivation" which he believed might underlie some persisting social problems. In the discussions and initiatives which sprang from this concept the idea of a national policy of "preparation for parenthood" was put forward and a seminar attended by the Secretaries of State for Social Services and Education was held in April 1973 at All Souls College, Oxford. The purpose of this seminar was "to expose to the rigour of searching academic scrutiny ideas which had been (assembled) about the role of parents, the quality of parenting and the scope for helping people in their parental role." Many dimensions of parenthood were considered under the guidance of distinguished speakers from Britain and the USA and the papers were subsequently published to stimulate discussion.[6] Opening the seminar the chairman[7] said: "The parenting of human beings is highly complex and demands a high degree of skill. Here is an attempt to suggest briefly some of these roles which offer parents and children emotional security, learning opportunities and a system of values which provides for a creative relationship with the larger society.'' She went on to outline what might be held to be characteristic of a family home if it were functioning effectively. Such a home

offers adequate shelter, space, food, income and the basic amenities which enable the adults to perform their marital, child-rearing and citizenship roles without incurring so much stress that anxiety inhibits a confident and positive performance;

secures the physical care, safety and healthy development of children either through its own resources or through the competent use of specialized help and services;

acknowledges its task of socializing children, encouraging their personal development and abilities, guiding their behaviour and interests and informing their attitudes and values;

offers the experience of warm, loving intimate and consistently dependable relationships;

assures the mother of support and understanding, particularly during the early child-rearing period, and provides the child with a male/father/husband model which continues to remain important through adolescence;

offers children an experience (2-6 years) of group life, so extending their social relationships, their awareness of others and intellectual development;

responds to children's curiosity with affection and reasoned explanation, and respects children through all developmental stages as persons in their own right, so securing affection and respect for others within the family circle and wider social network;

cooperates with school, values educational and learning opportunities, and encourages exploration and a widening experience;

supports adolescents physically and emotionally while they are achieving relative independence of the family, personal identity, sexual maturity, a work role, relationships within society and the testing out of values and ideologies;

provides a fall-back supportive system for the young married during their child-bearing period.

The seminar as a whole was not concerned with children who had had, for whatever reason, to leave their families, but with the needs of children living in their own families and with the promotion of family life as a natural setting for the fulfilment of dependent young human beings' needs in the first two decades or so of their lives. Nevertheless the characteristics of an effectively functioning family home outlined above provide the positive aspects of many of the issues raised by the negative experiences of the ten people in this book.

Parenting human beings may be seen as highly complex or basically simple, though either way it makes great demands, as any parent knows. It may be particularly demanding when the parenting must be provided by people other than the natural parents. Looking back on their lives, the people in this book identified many features of the parenting service they received which were less than adequate from their point of view. They recognized that they may have been extra sensitive compared with children in their own homes but they were "in a mesmerized state", suffering from shock; hurt and anxious, and worried about the future. They did not think they were helped by the additional, often unexplained losses of adults and children because "everyone seemed to be on the move". They felt "different" not just because of their personal situation but often because they were made to feel "different" by services and people; some felt they were being punished and rejected; they believed their families had a sense of stigma, and so had they. The need that every child has for a "special person" to talk to, to cling on to, in their case was not easily met because of insufficient individual attention in children's Homes, sometimes mistaken choices of foster homes or over use of willing foster homes so that children lost the attention and security they might have expected to enjoy. There was too little continuity, too much fragmentation, they had a sense of damaged identity, feelings of helplessness and isolation in the face of events and people taking charge of them, they felt they lost their childhood before they had lived through it, that bits of them were left behind, including relationships with residential staff and other children to whom they became attached but whom they never saw again when the moment came for them to move on. More specifically they had lacked sufficient opportunities to talk to someone about how they felt in any given situation, they had lacked the response from adults which would have allowed them to explain, even if they were in the wrong; they did not always know how or to whom to complain if they felt they had been unjustly treated or wanted an explanation of the mysterious, "illogical" way that things happened. They wanted to know more about themselves; sometimes their parents would not tell them, sometimes the public authority did not tell them or did not know. They felt 'retarded' in their general development, younger than they really were, though they seemed to have lost their youth. They felt their education had lacked the interest, encouragement, even compulsion, which were needed; and in consequence their whole working life, and therefore their own children and their later family life were affected, to their detriment. They knew from experience that for the outsider to know fully what is happening in someone else's house, whether it is a children's Home, a foster home, or a child's own home is very difficult and because of this they had needed much closer relationships with their social workers than their social workers offered, because they in their turn often appeared to be too detached, too "official" or too superficial. The motivations of foster parents, in their experience, were mixed. The difficulties of making and maintaining close and lasting relationships in any setting, for them, were great, though they needed such relationships to be able to communicate, and to be able to communicate was the key to so much more that they wanted but did not always receive. "Every child yearns for individual attention" they said; "I wanted to feel a whole person"; "nothing is ever completely yours"; they saw the years between leaving school and the mid-twenties as "the hardest part of one's life, when you are just finding your feet and beginning to realize what the big outside world is all about." They clearly felt positively about some, perhaps a majority, of their experiences of the child care service or they might not have been prepared to give so much of their time and themselves in discussion. They, themselves, were positive people who, in the main, were succeeding in general living. Yet the picture that emerged, in spite of this and the efforts made by the department concerned to provide adequately for them, was one which revealed much that might have greatly improved the substitute home provision being offered if it had been understood and incorporated at the time. Some of the problems that have to be faced by children in care can never be wholly compensated for, like desertion, death or rejection, but this fact should never be allowed to obscure the need to provide as sensitive and as adequate compensation as possible in the light of current knowledge and experience, and current knowledge can be increased by consultation with consumers, however young.

In summing up the Seminar on Dimensions of Parenthood, referred to earlier, both the chairman and the rapporteur spoke of the need to obtain consumer views. The chairman suggested that 'lay involvement in social systems needed to increase rather than decrease if the authority gap between providers and users of systems was not to be increased.' The rapporteur[8] commented:

The parents' views might or might not coincide with the views of "the experts". But it should not be overlooked that so far, the people who have not been consulted are the parents themselves, actual or prospective. Such strategies are not as fanciful in 1973 as they would have been ten years ago; they are consonant with trends in community work of various kinds and with ideals of citizen participation. In many ways, this creates new problems, of finding out what is wanted, of deciding when and when not to follow the suggestions, of finding resources to meet the demands and so on. However, one can be almost certain that schemes which are soundly based on the self-perceived needs of parents are more likely to succeed.

In any case, it seems the least we can do in order to affirm our respect for their status.

Children in care and young people recently out of care are prospective parents and have, in addition, experienced first hand the services for children whose parents cannot care for them.

Since 1973, as has been shown earlier, numbers of children in long-term care have risen and continue to rise. The numbers of children requiring long-term substitute parenting are considerable, and include a growing number of older children and young people, who, in spite of valuable developments in fostering, present more problems in satisfactory placement than younger or tiny children. For many years now it has been part of social work thinking to recognize that children who cannot be with their own parents nevertheless still need them, and that it is difficult and often undesirable for anyone else to try to take their place. This has led to a professional approach in one form of substitute care, residential work, which was expressed in 1969 as follows:

The majority of children in care have parents with whom they are encouraged to keep in touch and even when this is not so, they remember them or are being helped to prepare for acceptance of foster parents or adopters. Either way residential staff cannot, by the nature of their role, provide substitute parental relationships; they can and should provide warm, supportive and enabling relationships and treatment within the structure of a therapeutic community. This is the nature of their professional task.[9]

Similarly, since the early 1950s it has been commonly accepted that foster parents need to be able to accept a child's own parents and to maintain the balance between providing substitute parenting and not usurping the natural parents' place.

Adopters, though legally taking over the rights of natural parents, have also been advised and helped to respect their child's need to know about his natural origins and not to deny the complexity of his and their relationships.

At best these approaches to children's needs have provided sensitive understanding of their conflicting loyalties, support for their separation grief and for their gradual readjustment and coming to terms with either prolonged separation or eventual return to their parent or parents. They will continue to receive professional support and implementation and there is plenty of evidence to show that, however deprived of their natural parents, many children deeply resent and reject attempts to supplant them. The feelings expressed by Anne to her fellow group members were only one clear example of this.

On the other hand it is regrettably easy for a substantially based aspect of theory and good practice to produce a converse swing too far in the opposite direction, especially when it may be imperfectly understood or applied. Such a swing can be seen in the views held by some practising staff that children should not be encouraged/allowed to make short-term relationships in, for example, observation and assessment centres, nursery care and other short-term provision, that they can be satisfied with group care that provides for basic essentials but does not develop individual attachments and that multiple moves, while regrettable, can be sustained without too much damage. These views fail to take adequately into account the fine balance that lies between loyalty and need for blood ties, and the day-to-day need of young people for the comfort, support, dependability, acceptance and long-term nature of the relationships which parents normally provide in effectively functioning family homes,[10] and which, when they do not, must be supplied elsewhere if the child or young person is to have "emotional security, learning opportunities and a system of values which provides for a creative relationship with the larger society."[11]

The ten people whose discussions have been recorded here were talking of experiences between 1942 and 1969. There have been indications in the years since 1970 that long-term childhood needs are still inadequately met for some children in care. At one end of the spectrum are the securely and happily adopted or fostered children and young people, or those who are happy and secure in their children's Home.

Little is heard about them and comparatively little is known. At the other end of the spectrum are those with such acute problems that extreme measures appear to be necessary to deal with them. The increase in demand for secure accommodation for children in care illustrates this end of the spectrum. Secure accommodation was one of the measures envisaged by the Children & Young Persons Act, 1969, as being needed in extreme situations when it might be necessary either to protect a child or young person from the consequences of his own behaviour or to protect society against him, and in either case that it might on occasion be used even though it was not necessarily primarily in the interests of his welfare. Apart from a few geographically widely spaced secure units pre-1971, and single secure rooms in the former approved schools, this kind of accommodation has been provided and used since 1971, and until recently little information about its use and the children and young persons in it has been available. Recently however, a major research study [12] has shed some light on the use made of the units, the children and young people in them and how they got there. It comments as follows:

The reading of several hundred voluminous files on secure unit children is a sobering experience. They are an indictment of the child-care system. Children are shuffled from one short-term placement to another in the vague hope that they will stick somewhere. Some boys have had eight placements in a year . . . They return occasionally to assessment centres for additional uncomplimentary labels and then they are on their way again. They find the experience disintegrating . . . . Not only is placement haphazard; it seems to be based on a series of panic responses. There is certainly no unifying treatment concept. . . . Most boys in the units have considerable experience of all forms of residential care . . . . their experience of closed provision in the penal system, too, is quite extensive.

Most of the boys were found to be only thirteen years old and in a foreword to the published study *Locking Up Children,*

Roy Parker asks,

Who are the children considered to require secure accommodation? Does their behaviour differ in a pronounced fashion from that of other children living in community homes? ... Few differences are found to exist between boys in these two groups. Might not the reasons for a boy arriving in security be found instead in social service interventions at earlier stages, and, particularly, by looking at the kinds of circumstances which give rise to referral and acceptance?

Children and young persons in secure accommodation, even young persons in the prisons and borstals, are, and are likely to continue to be, a relatively small minority of those in care, but they are a signal indication in many cases of how fragmentation of a life can lead to loss of self-regard, confused personal identity, depression, alienation and loss of confidence in the future. These feelings, regrettably, may influence the young people concerned long after they are free from the confines of their secure care accommodation.

The ten people in this book, even years later, found the movement of other people and the changes that happened to them difficult to accept. They regretted the number of different social workers to whom they had to relate. Their feelings were mirrored by the 'Who Cares' Young People's Working Group which gave a more extreme picture:

My brother and I have had more social workers than I can remember. They'd see us once and then disappear for six months, then we'd have a new one. And it's been going on all the time I've been in the home. They've been leaving or they've been going ill. And if that's happening all the time, I don't see how they can help you.

It's the coming and going that hurts. The first time you move to another place it hurts bad so you build up a shell but one day the shell cracks.[13]

(Andrew used the image of a hard shell sixteen years after going out of care to describe his attempts to deal with change and its accompanying losses.)

A detailed comparison of how the two groups expressed their feelings and described their experiences would show a number of other close parallels. The areas of discussion in which there were few parallels were those concerning discipline, punishment and violence. The ten people talking in 1970 recalled some threats, some physical punishments and some disciplinary practices which they saw as unjust, unkind and unlikely to benefit children in care, but these incidents did not feature widely in their discussions. Nor did they appear to have accepted, as the editors suggest the "Who Cares" Young People's Working Group had, the "effectiveness of violence". The "Who Cares" group in 1976 were said by the editors to be:

practised in identifying inconsistencies, contradictions and hypocrisies in adult behaviour and beliefs. They knew that a parent or someone acting in a parent's place could treat a child in a way in which it would not be politic to treat another adult. Children were naturally "on the receiving end". They knew too that in approving a reasonable level of corporal punishment society has not established a fail-safe sanction against abuse and that abuse was not always remote from children who had to live in care. Many of the members of our group knew they were in care because they had been ill-treated by their parents. It was a paradox to them to find that they could also be ill-treated in care.[14]

In their conclusions the editors add:

When we first began meeting, all the adults in the group were concerned that so ready an acceptance of physical violence should be seen by our group as natural to the life of children, even though many of the young people had themselves been ill-treated by their parents. . . . Over the next year all the young people questioned the wisdom of relying on corporal punishment as a method of controlling children in care. As one boy concluded, "There are other ways besides hitting and shouting". Increasingly our group expressed concern for all children in care and many found younger children who had been ill-treated confiding in them. . . . Again our group have illustrated why children in care find it extremely difficult to confide in adults. To discuss your feelings and concerns, particularly if you are being ill-treated, is a risky enterprise. The only adults to whom you have access are grown-ups with power over both your day-to-day life and future. If the adults prove unreliable or unworthy of your trust, you stand to lose all.[15]

Add the concerns thus expressed to the natural trauma of losing family, home and security, accompanied by the confusion, inability to control explosive feelings and fears of the unpredictable, and the mixture may begin to provide a recipe for disaster, for the use of extreme measures like secure accommodation, for a long-term future prejudiced by the events of a disadvantaged, deprived childhood.

There are indications above that, although the ten people talking in 1970 were a small, unrepresentative group looking back and remembering with the gaps and distortions which memory may have suffered, nevertheless many of the things that were important to them are important to many others in 1979 and are likely to continue to be important to children and young people who cannot be with their own parents during the years when they need them most. In spite of indications that they could be helpful, may even be significant in the success of certain kinds of social policies, consumers' views are still insufficiently canvassed, or taken into account, in policy making, deployment of staff and methods of care and social work currently used.

It is well known that bad news finds a readier audience than good news, and that failure and difficulties in the personal social services receive more publicity, even more investigation, than the positive achievements. Amongst the community there must be a very large number of ex-children in care who are now living their lives, rearing their children and carrying forward with them, as we all do, the experiences they had when they were children. They may have important news to offer, good and bad, with lessons that should be learned by policy makers, professional service providers, training agencies and the public as a whole. There is evidence that they might be willing to tell us the news. Should we not give them the opportunity?

References

PREFACE

1. Eileen Younghusband, *Social Work in Britain 1950-1975*, George Allen & Unwin, 1978.
2. P.G. Gray and Elizabeth Parr, *Children in Care and the Recruitment of Foster Parents*, Social Survey S.S. 249. November 1957.
3. Jean Packman, *Child Care: Needs & Numbers*, George Allen & Unwin, 1968.
4. *Children in Care in England & Wales, March 1977*, HMSO, 1979.
5. *Report of the Care of Children Committee*, Cmd 6922, HMSO, 1946, para 1.
6. Younghusband, *Social Work in Britain*, p. 50.
7. Wordworth's preface to *Lyrical Ballads*, 1798.
8. 'Who Cares?' National Children's Bureau Conference, June 1975.
9. *Who Cares? Young People in Care Speak Out*, ed. Raissa Page and G.A. Clark, National Children's Bureau, 1977, p. 10.

CHAPTER 1

1. *Report of the Committee on Local Authority and Allied Personal Social Services*, 1968, Cmnd 3703. Known as the Seebohm Committee.
2. *Report of the Committee on Care of Children & Young Persons*, 1946, Cmd 6922. Known as the Curtis Committee.
3. Ibid. para 429.

4.   Lady Allen of Hurtwood, in particular, mounted a record correspondence in *The Times* starting with her letter on July 5th, 1944. This letter strongly criticized existing methods of care for deprived children and stated that "a Public Inquiry, with full government support, is urgently needed."

5.   Monckton Inquiry into the death of Dennis O'Neill, 1945.

6.   Children Act, 1948.

7.   Cmd 6922, para 441.

8.   Ibid.

9.   Reported in *The Times,* 29 June 1948.

10. *Training in Child Care: Interim Report of the Care of Children Committee,* Cmd 6760, para 1, 1945.

11. Packman, *Child Care: Needs & Numbers.*

12. Ibid. p. 191.

13. Examples of legislation were the Children & Young Persons (Amendment) Act, 1952, the Children & Young Persons Act, 1963 and the Adoption Acts, 1958.

14. Jean Packman, *The Child's Generation, Child Care Policy from Curtis to Houghton,* Blackwell & Robertson, 1975, p.1.

15. Ibid.

16. Ibid. p. 42.

17. Ibid. p. 56.

18. Ibid. p. 30.

CHAPTER   5

1.   *Training in Child Care: Interim Report of the Care of Children Committee,* Cmd 6760.

2.   Ibid. para 10.

3.   Packman, *The Child's Generation,* p. 39.

4.   Ibid. p. 39.

CHAPTER   6

1.   *Report of the Care of Children Committee,* Cmd 6922, September 1946. Recommendation 33: 'Reception centres should be set up in all areas and should serve as places of safety, remand homes for small children and places of

preparation for boarding out or the children's Home.' See paras 482-483.
2. Ibid. para 482. 'We do not think observation should last for more than a few weeks at the outside.'
3. Children Act, 1948, section 19.

CHAPTER 7

1. *Report of the Care of Children Committee,* Cmd 6922, para 448.
2. Ibid. para 460.
3. Ibid. para 461.
4. Children Act, 1948, section 13.1. (a) and (b).
5. Cmd 6922, para 369.
6. Ibid. para 370.
7. Examples of these are G. Trasler, *In Place of Parents,* Routledge & Kegan Paul, 1960 and R.A. Parker, *Decision in Child Care. A Study of Prediction in Fostering,* Allen & Unwin, 1966.
8. Children & Young Persons Act, 1969, section 13.1.
9. The Boarding-Out of Children Regulations, 1955.

CHAPTER 8

1. *Report of the Care of Children Committee,* Cmd 6922, para 348.
2. Ibid. para 443.
3. Ibid. para 443.
4. Ibid. para 445.

EPILOGUE

1. The changes which took place in 1974 included a legal obligation on both the NHS and local authorities to collaborate. N.H.S. Reorganisation Act, 1973, Sec. 11. (3).
2. Children and Young Persons Act, 1969, and Chronically Sick and Disabled Act, 1970.

3. 'Who Cares?' Young People in Care Speak Out, National Children's Bureau Conference, 1975, and report of Young People's Working Group, 1977.
4. 'Supervision and Intermediate Treatment', February 1976. Obtainable from Room 1104, Alexander Fleming House, Elephant and Castle, London SE 1. 'Caring for Adolescents in Kent,' an unpublished report.
5. *Children in Care in England and Wales, March 1977,* HMSO, 1979.
6. *The Family in Society: Dimensions of Parenthood,* HMSO, 1974.
7. Miss Joan D. Cooper, CB, then Director of the Social Work Service, Department of Health and Social Security.
8. Professor Olive Stevenson.
9. *Residential Task in Child Care,* The Castle Priory Report, 1969. ed. Barbara Kahan and Geoffrey Banner, para 16.
10. *The Family in Society,* p. 12.
11. Ibid. p. 11.
12. Spencer Millham, Roger Bullock and Kenneth Hosie, *Locking Up children,* Saxon House, 1978.
13. 'Who Cares': Children in Care Speak Out, p. 35.
14. Ibid. p. 35.
15. Ibid. p. 59.

Index

197